I0520823

Midwestern Miscellany

LIII
Issue 2
FALL
2025

1925

Guest Editor

Scott D. Emmert

The Midwestern Press

Copy Editing and Design
Patricia Oman

Midwestern Miscellany (ISSN 0885-4742) is a peer-reviewed journal published
twice a year (Spring and Fall) by The Society for the Study of Midwestern Literature.

The journal is a member of the Council of Editors of Learned Journals.

In honor of

Roger Bresnahan

2026 MidAmerica Award Recipient

CONTENTS

PREFACE

Scott D. Emmert

The year 1925 stands out in American literature for the large number of distinguished works that saw print that year. One hundred years later, this issue of *Midwestern Miscellany* recognizes the contributions of midwestern authors to this significant cultural moment by re-examining canonical novels and by discussing others that have received less notice.

John Rohrkemper opens the issue with an essay on three well-known novels: *The Sun Also Rises*, which Ernest Hemingway began in 1925, and Willa Cather's *The Professor's House* and F. Scott Fitzgerald's *The Great Gatsby*, which were published in 1925. Rohrkemper situates each novel within the era's racial fixations to illuminate cultural anxieties about national identity that were "always framed in terms of race." In the essay that follows, David Buehrer applies two conceptions of nostalgia within a close reading of *The Great Gatsby* to argue for Nick's complex engagement with his "Middle West" in contrast to Gatsby's more stagnant nostalgic response to his past.

In the next essay, Marilyn Judith Atlas writes about two lesser-known novels that Floyd Dell published in 1925. Examining *This Mad Ideal* and *Runaway*, Atlas elucidates Dell's modern, and modernist, treatment of "women's bodily autonomy, sexuality, creativity, and [ideas about] marriage" (35). Appearing next is an essay by Robert Beasecker that unearths two Michigan novels about farm life: G. D. Eaton's *Backfurrow* and John T. Frederick's *Green Bush*. Beasecker demonstrates the importance of each novel within the genre of farm literature and details their distinctive contributions to an understanding of rural midwestern experience in the early twentieth century.

The issue concludes with my essay on H. L. Mencken's reviews of midwestern books published in 1925 to document his promotion of midwestern writers to a national readership. Together these essays evoke the richness in books from

1925 by midwestern authors, and they suggest the rewards of continuing to read and study them.

University of Wisconsin—Oshkosh

UNDER THE RED, WHITE, AND BLUE

Americanism, Nativism, and Antisemitism in *The Sun Also Rises, The Professor's House*, and *The Great Gatsby*

John Rohrkemper

James Woodress has called the year 1925 "the *annus mirabilis* of American litera-ture," and certainly it was a remarkable year, especially in fiction (353). It saw the publication of Theodore Dreiser's *An American Tragedy*, Ellen Glasgow's *Barren Ground*, Ernest Hemingway's *In Our Time*, Sinclair Lewis's *Arrowsmith,* John Dos Passos's *Manhattan Transfer*, Anita Loos's *Gentlemen Prefer Blondes*, and Gertrude Stein's *The Making of Americans*. Farther afield, 1925 marked the publication of Virginia Woolf's *Mrs. Dalloway*, Ford Maddox Ford's *No More Parades*, André Gide's *The Counterfeiters*, and Franz Kafka's *The Trial*. It was an exceptional year for modern literature. Two of the three works that will be examined here—F. Scott Fitzgerald's *The Great Gatsby* and Willa Cather's *The Professor's House* also appeared in 1925; the third, Ernest Hemingway's *The Sun Also Rises*, was published in 1926 but Hemingway began drafting the novel in 1925. All three works, published within months of each other, have endured as central texts in the American modernist canon. They are time-tested as we might say, but they also are works very much of their time, the first years of the 1920s. There perhaps are many ways these three novels might be said to be of their time, but I would like to examine here one specific context for considering these novels together: each responds to an American preoccupation in pre- and post-war America with the effects of eighty years of intense immigration, a rising interest in the pseudo-science of eugenics, a concern for the racial purity of the American stock, and a racist backlash against Eastern and Southern Europeans as supposed polluters of that stock. This American preoccupation is not necessarily the preoccupation of any of these novels, but each resonates with what was, at that moment, a vociferous and sometimes furious debate about what America is and was. And what it should be. And this debate was always framed in terms of race.

From the first confrontation of Europeans with Indigenous people to the subsequent enslavement of Black Africans, America has been about race. From the Trail of Tears to the Tulsa Massacre, from Nat Turner to Leonard Peltier, from the Carlisle Indian Industrial School to the barred schoolhouse door, from Japanese internment camps to Alligator Alcatraz, America has been about race. But while we may easily characterize the relationships between Euro-Americans, Indigenous peoples, African Americans, Asian Americans, and perhaps even Latin Americans as racial, American thinking about race has often been more complicated. The so-called science of race really began in the eighteenth century. Benjamin Franklin, in his *Observations Concerning the Increase of Mankind*, contemplated the ways that Pennsylvania in the mid-eighteenth century was changing as the result of a wave of German immigration to the colony. He wrote,

> Why should Pennsylvania, founded by the English, become a colony of *Aliens*, who will shortly be so numerous as to Germanize us instead of our Anglifying them, and will never adopt our Language or Customs, any more than they can acquire our complexion? (qtd. in Morgan 77, italics in original)

Note that Franklin is addressing not merely differences in language and custom but also specifically differences of color, of what he considers race. We, perhaps, find it strange that Franklin would note significant differences between the *complexions* of those of English and German stock, but Edmund S. Morgan, in his biography of Franklin, points out that, in Franklin's racialized view,

> Most of the world was peopled by men and women of darker skin than the English: Africa by blacks, Asia and America (before the English came) by the "tawny" colored. Even most Europeans were "generally of

what we call a swarthy Complexion," including most Germans, except for the Saxons from whom the English were descended. (77)

Franklin's observations clearly illustrate the point raised by Ta-Nehisi Coates and many others that "race is the child of racism," that the need to classify people by their supposed differences and place them in a precise hierarchy of value is the result of ideology, not objective science, that racism preceded the social construct of race (7). By the first decades of the twentieth century, Franklin's odd ideas about what constituted race hadn't really dissipated. If anything, they had been given greater currency by the apparently scientific nature of race study. In the first decades of the century there was a flood of books, pamphlets, speeches, and articles that sounded an increasing din of eugenic nativism, clamoring to shut the door to potential immigrants, and sounding the warning alarm about those already arrived, particularly recently, especially those "swarthier" arrivals: Russian and Polish Jews, Italians, Portuguese, and Greeks. Such titles as John L. Brandt's *Anglo-Saxon Supremacy; Or, Race Contributions to Civilization* (1915), C. B. Davenport's "The Effects of Race Intermingling" (1917), Charles W. Gould's *America: A Family Matter* (1922), and Clinton Stoddard Burr's *America's Race Heritage* (1922) were among many other works that sounded the alarm.

Eugenicists had an expansive view of race and typically divided Europeans into several supposed races: Nordics, Alpines, and Mediterraneans, sometimes adding the more specific designations of Levantines and Hebraics. Each group, or race, supposedly had its own racial characteristics. The Nordic "race," comprising Great Britain, Scandinavia, parts of Finland and Russia, the Netherlands, northern Germany, and parts of northern France, supposedly had the superior characteristics, making them supreme in intelligence and valor, leadership, and initiative. Immigration was at least diluting the Nordic hegemony and, in eugenicists' most fearsome nightmare, threatened to obliterate Nordic values and bloodlines in an alien tidal wave.

It is important to keep in mind that these ideas were not the rantings of a rabid fringe or merely the province of some obscure academic debating societies. Such discussions of race, ethnicity, and immigration policy were an important part of the intellectual temperature of the first decades of the century; they were front-page news. These works sold well and were published by some of the most prestigious publishing houses and in some of the leading periodicals of the time. For instance, it was in *The Proceedings of the American Philosophical Society* that C. B. Davenport warned of "The Effects of Race Intermingling." Here's one more example that suggests the popularity of such ideas, a 1921 article entitled "Whose Country Is This?" that warned of the danger of Nordic Americans succumbing to immigrant hordes. The author of this article was then–Vice-President Calvin Coolidge, and it appeared in that not-so-obscure periodical *Good Housekeeping*.

More than a decade of eugenic proselytizing culminated in the 1920s. In 1921, the year of Coolidge's article, the United States enacted, with all but one vote in both houses of Congress, the Emergency Quota Act, the most comprehensive immigration law to that date, and the first to use rigid national quotas, based on the census of 1910, to control immigration. This act was replaced three years later by the Johnson-Reed Act of 1924, which continued the quotas, but tightened them and tied them, not to the 1910 census as the Emergency Quota Act had, but to the 1890 census, which documented a period before the heavy influx of immigrants from Eastern and Southern Europe. The consequences were dramatic, keeping the door open for immigration by so-called Nordic people, but virtually slamming the door on "undesirable" Alpines and Mediterraneans, i.e., Southern and Eastern Europeans: Italian and Portuguese Catholics, Greek Orthodox Christians, and Russian and Polish Jews. Clearly, the Johnson-Reed Act was designed to prevent the United States from becoming what Quentin Compson in another 1920s novel characterized as "the land of the kike, home of the wop" (Faulkner 125).

Two of the most influential eugenicist works, Madison Grant's *The Passing of the Great Race; Or, The Racial Basis of European History* (1916) and Lothrop Stoddard's *The Rising Tide of Color Against White World-Supremacy* (1920), were published by Charles Scribner's Sons and edited by Maxwell Perkins. Perkins today is known as the editor and confidant of several masters of American modernism, including Fitzgerald and Hemingway. It is less well known that at essentially the same time he was the editor for eugenicists such as Grant, Stoddard, and others. In the opinion of Ian Frazier, from the mid-teens to the mid-thirties, Scribner's was "the leading purveyor of white-supremacist books in the United States" (par. 13).

Many of the eugenicists were of noteworthy social and intellectual standing. Madison Grant, scion of an old New York family, was by training a biologist and anthropologist. He is considered one of the founders of the conservation movement in this country, earning great credit for his efforts to save the American Bison from extinction, for helping to establish several national parks, and for founding The Bronx Zoo. In his preface to *The Passing of the Great Race*, Henry Fairfield Osborn, an eminent paleontologist and president of the American Museum of Natural History, called Grant's work a "hereditary interpretation of history" and asserted with brio that "[t]here is no gainsaying that this is the correct scientific method of approaching the problem of the past" (Grant viii). Lothrop Stoddard was a blue-blooded Bostonian, a Harvard-trained historian and lawyer. He was a prominent member of numerous academic societies and was an active member of the Birth Control League, the forerunner of Planned Parenthood. He was also a member of and an advisor to the Ku Klux Klan (Yudell 41–44). In his *The Rising Tide of Color Against White World-Supremacy*, he states the eugenicist's case against the new immigrants:

> Our country, originally settled almost exclusively by Nordics, was toward the close of the nineteenth century invaded by hordes of immigrant Alpines and Mediterraneans, not to mention Asiatic elements such as Levantines and Jews. As a result, the Nordic native American has been crowded out with amazing rapidity by these swarming, prolific aliens, and after two short generations he has in many of our urban areas become almost extinct. (165)

It should be noted that in the post-war world, American ideas had more currency than they had had previously. American eugenicists were heard overseas.

Adolph Hitler read *The Passing of the Great Race* in translation, admired what Grant had to say about the "Nordic race," and wrote the author a flattering letter, calling the book "my Bible" (Frazier par. 8). The future Fuhrer would soon publish another noteworthy book of 1925—*Mein Kampf*. Furthermore, seventeen years after the appearance of *The Passing of the Great Race*, Grant, working again with Perkins and Scribner's, published another race book, *The Conquest of a Continent; Or, The Expansion of Races in America*. It was 1933, the year Hitler came to and consolidated his power in Germany. A promotional piece from Scribner's touting the book argued that "national problems are today, at bottom, race problems. Herr Hitler has stated the problem for Germany—and is working out his own solution. We in America have our own problem" (qtd. in Okrent 368). This, then, is the atmosphere, the American zeitgeist, in which *The Sun Also Rises*, *The Professor's House*, and *The Great Gatsby* were written and read.

The Sun Also Rises, of course, is set wholly outside the United States, but its most prominent characters are either American or British—the one nationality that Franklin could consider white, what the eugenicists called Nordic. There is an exception to this, however. Significantly, Jake Barnes, the novel's protagonist and narrator, begins his story by discussing his ineffectual nemesis, Robert Cohn:

> Robert Cohn was once middleweight boxing champion of Princeton. Do not think I am very much impressed by that as a boxing title, but it meant a lot to Cohn. He cared nothing for boxing, in fact he disliked it, but he learned it painfully and thoroughly to counteract the feeling of being treated as a Jew at Princeton. There was a certain inner comfort in knowing he could knock down anybody who was snooty to him, although, being very shy and a thoroughly nice boy, he never fought except in the gym. (5)

What might seem to be a rather objective and neutral introduction to Cohn's background in fact begins to stack the deck against him. In this novel that is so centrally concerned with establishing what really matters, where true value resides in a world shattered by the Great War, our narrator tells us that he is not very impressed with what "meant a lot" to Cohn. Furthermore, Cohn, who "cared nothing about boxing," lacks the passion for the contest that takes place in his ring as compared to the *afición* displayed by the true artists of the bullring later in the novel. Finally, in this novel about rebellion against accepted pieties, Cohn is characterized dismissively as a "thoroughly nice boy."

Protagonists often need foils, but in this case, the dominance of Jake's narrative voice makes his characterization of Cohn seem like bullying. And the fact that there is no necessity for Barnes's foil to be Jewish or for his heritage to be remarked upon, as it so often is, makes Jake's antisemitic comments seem particularly gratuitous. Cohn isn't merely a foil for Barnes; he's the easy stereotype, the comic other. We are told on the novel's first page that the broken nose that Cohn suffered in the ring at Princeton "certainly improved his nose," playing on a gratuitous, antisemitic trope (5). When Robert tries to enlist Jake in his plan to go to South America and is at first unwilling to accept Jake's refusal to go with him, we are told that Cohn "had a hard, Jewish, stubborn streak" (10). When Robert first sees Jake's friend and would-be lover, Lady Brett, he "looked a great deal as his compatriot must have looked when he saw the promised land" (18). (I wonder if the Catholic Barnes would have referred to St. Paul or Augustine as "his compatriot.") Jake's semitic references decrease as the novel progresses, as Cohn's weakness and ineffectualness are made manifest by his own behavior, but by then Barnes has established the "Jewishness" of Cohn's unattractive traits and behavior. Donald Daiker points out that most of the antisemitic comments directed toward Cohn come from two characters, Mike Campbell and Bill Gorton, both of whom spout a lot of nonsense about many things throughout the novel. He notes that Jake never articulates aloud an antisemitic smear (44). Nevertheless, by focusing the two opening chapters of the novel on Jake's analysis of Cohn's often unattractive attitudes and behavior, and seemingly linking them to his Jewishness, Hemingway frames the novel antisemitically.

It wasn't always necessarily going to be that way. Hemingway's original plan was to begin the novel at the fiesta in Pamplona and perhaps make the young matador, Pedro Romero, the novel's protagonist. And the final draft of the novel begins with a brief and amusing biography of Brett, including her relationship with her two husbands and now with Mike Campbell. The opening words of this draft might suggest that Brett will be the novel's protagonist: "This is a novel about a lady. Her name is Lady Ashley" (Svoboda 131). It was only in the second chapter that Jake turned his attention to Cohn. Either beginning might have deflected some of the unsavory effects of focusing on Cohn's Jewishness from the onset. When Hemingway received the galley proofs, however, he struck out the entire first chapter and the first part of the second, picking up where the novel ultimately begins, with the unflattering portrait of Cohn and his Jewishness (Svoboda 131–37). Also struck were two references to Cohn in terms made popular by the eugenics movement. In the deleted section of Chapter Two, Jake refers to Robert Cohn as "non-Nordic" and "un-Nordic" (Svoboda 135, 136). Neither specific reference is particularly unflattering in context, but they do suggest Hemingway's awareness, perhaps internalization, of eugenic thinking about race, though I could also entertain the idea that these subtle references to the eugenicists are intended to be a way of satirizing them. Whatever Hemingway's intent, it is interesting to consider the irony of the fact that two of the novel's most positive characters, the innkeeper Montoya and the matador Pedro Romero, had they wished to immigrate to the United States in 1923, the time setting of the novel, would have had a difficult time. They would probably have been prevented by the 1921 Emergency Quota Act. If they had decided to immigrate a year or two later, they would almost certainly have been excluded by the more draconian quotas of the Johnson-Reed Act.

After the gates of Auschwitz and Buchenwald and other death camps were broached by Allied troops in 1945, Hemingway may have been embarrassed by the easy antisemitism of *The Sun Also Rises*. But even if he had been so chastened, his chagrin would have come too late. It is dismaying—and very telling about the age in which the novel was written and first read—that, in this otherwise skillfully and meticulously crafted novel, Hemingway relies on such a cheap trick to establish his narrator's comparative heroism. But it was a cheap trick well prepared for by the racialized rhetoric of the xenophobic 1920s.

Willa Cather's writing, both her journalism and fiction, suggest that she was familiar with and perhaps somewhat influenced by eugenic thinking. In her breakthrough 1913 novel *O Pioneers!* Cather mused—through her protagonist, Alexandra—on the ethnically diverse types of immigrants that had settled on Nebraska's Divide. The way she describes the differences between the Scandinavian boys and the Bohemian boys and the French boys suggests she might have been thinking of them as inherently racial distinctions rather than merely learned cultural differences (110). And, more specifically, Jewish characters appear in several of Willa Cather's stories and novels. Lisa Marcus notes that Cather moved to New York City in 1906 and thus, "while Cather was casting her gaze westward, back to the Great Plains, she was also training her fictional eye on a far different landscape: the ethnic cityscape of the great American metropolis, teeming with newly arrived immigrants" (67). Marcus argues that Cather betrays a

> marked ambivalence that is manifested in two divergent types of characters: on the one hand, a grasping, ambitious Jewish figure, linked to New York City, who threatens to infect American culture with a crass commercialism and to taint the purity of the American family through miscegenation; and, on the other hand, a much less frequent figure in Cather's fiction, "the finest kind of Jews," cultured and intellectual, often second-generation German Jews as she encountered in the Midwest. (67–68)

The first type of Jewish character is personified in her short story "Scandal" by Siegmund Stein, an immigrant who has worked his way up from the sweatshops of New York to become the owner of one of the most prominent department stores in the city. When a celebrated opera diva agrees to perform for Stein's housewarming to placate a friend, she is repulsed by Stein's mostly Jewish guests, and the mansion becomes a sort of gothic house of horror in her imagination.

The Professor's House, written nearly a decade after "Scandal," examines the stereotype of the "grasping, ambitious" Jew with greater nuance than the earlier story. Louie Marsellus shares some of Stein's attributes when we first meet him in the novel. He is, indeed, initially presented to us as a gaudy, ostentatious materialist, seemingly blind to true value and bedazzled by a meretricious age. Marsellus is the son-in-law of Godfrey St. Peter, the professor of the novel's title. He is also presented as the antithesis of Tom Outland, a young man who had been St. Peter's intellectual and spiritual son. Outland, who tragically had been killed in the Great War, had earlier been a cowboy and had stumbled upon the ruins of the southwest's Blue Mesa Pueblo and had attempted to honor and preserve the relics of the ancient civilization that had once flourished there. Tom had been betrayed by a comrade who sold off those relics to foreign "collections." Perhaps St. Peter cannot quite suppress the feeling that Tom has again been betrayed when his daughter Rosamond, who had been Tom's fiancée, marries Louie Marsellus. Louie and Rosamond have gotten rich from the patent of one of Tom's inventions and their lavish lifestyle is an affront to the ascetic St. Peter. When they announce plans to build an ostentatious home with a shrine that will celebrate Outland's accomplishments, the gaudy excess of the project seems to the professor to add insult to injury.

In the early section of the novel in which Louie is introduced, we are subjected to what seems the obligatory ethnic detail of his physiognomy, here rendered in a metaphor that is uncharacteristically awkward for Cather:

> There was nothing Semitic about his countenance except his nose—
> that took the lead. It was not at all an unpleasing feature, but it grew out
> of his face with masterful strength, well-rooted, like a vigorous oak-tree
> growing out of a hill-side. (43)

But Louie is a more multi-faceted and nuanced character than he might at first seem. On balance, St. Peter is disapproving of Louie's crass materialism, but, then again, he's critical of the same characteristic in the other members of his family and the larger culture as well. He does blame Louie for his part in what he perceives as a change in his family, for the way Rosamond and his wife, Lillian, have become "hardened" by their materialism. At one point, St. Peter accompanies Rosamond to Chicago to shop for new furnishings for the palatial new home, but he comes home early, his head spinning from Rosamond's rapacious buying spree. While he holds Louie—who indulges his wife's materialistic whims—partly to blame, he also comes to realize that Louie has been able to retain a generosity that leads him to use his wealth to benefit others. When Augusta, the woman who makes clothing for the St. Peter women and mother-hens the professor, loses most of her life savings in an unwise investment, St. Peter expresses his faith in Louie's generosity: "I'll speak to Louie [about Augusta's plight]. He's an absolutely generous chap. I've never known him to refuse to give either time or money" (130). In fact, as the novel progresses, Louie increasingly seems to be an essentially open, thoughtful, generous, forgiving, vital young man, who perhaps is somewhat but unintentionally abrasive and off-putting to the genteel professor and to their sleepy university town.

The novel's treatment of Louie's Judaism is different from Hemingway's treatment of Robert Cohn most importantly because Cather explores the culture of antisemitism that conspires to treat Louie and others like him as permanent outsiders—outlanders, if I may use that term. Lillian, who enjoys the company of her son-in-law, nevertheless sees him as essentially different, suggesting there is something "Oriental" about him, adopting a trope popularized by eugenicists when applied to Jews during that era to stress their difference from a perceived Nordic norm (48–69). St. Peter himself thinks of Louie as "exotic," even "foreign," even though there is no suggestion that he is not a native-born American (78).

Within the family it is the St. Peters' younger daughter Kitty and her husband Scott who are most inclined to betray a naked antisemitism in their dealings with Louie. They resent his wealth, the way he seemed to usurp Tom Outland's place in the family. Scott is underpaid and doing work that he neither likes nor values; Kitty is acutely aware of everything her sister can have that she must do without. When Kitty confides to St. Peter that she has come to hate her sister, he suggests that some of the strain between them is because Kitty has been "untactful about Louie." Kitty responds, "Even if I have, why should [Rosamond] be so revengeful? Does she think nobody else calls him a Jew? Does she think it's a secret? I don't mind being called a Gentile" (85). Later, when Louie tells Rosamond that he would like to offer a kindness to Scott and Kitty, his wife is scornful of his offer and cuts him by revealing that Scott had blocked Louie's membership in the town's exclusive Arts and Letters Society, presumably using Marsellus's Jewishness as his trump card. When St. Peter tries to apologize for his family's cruelty to him, Louie responds,

> Oh that's all right, sir. As for Scott, I can understand. He was the first son of the family and he was the whole thing. Then I came along, a stranger, and carried off Rosie, and this patent began to pay so well—it's enough to make any man jealous…. But I think Scott will come around in the end; people usually do if you treat them well, and I mean to. I like the fellow. (170)

To this St. Peter can only exclaim, "Louie, you are magnanimous and magnificent," in offering a final assessment of Marsellus (170).

When we first meet Louie Marsellus in *The Professor's House*, he seems to tend toward caricature as Robert Cohn does, but perhaps because both Hemingway and Cather are so committed to their craft both characters become more complex as the novels progress, particularly Louie. And certainly, *The Professor's House* acknowledges the casual antisemitism that typified the era, but, ultimately, the novel offers at least a mild rebuke to such attitudes and presents a character who is human in his foibles and his gifts.

Neither *The Sun Also Rises* nor *The Professor's House* makes explicit reference to the eugenics movement; Fitzgerald's novel does. Since Maxwell Perkins

edited some of the principal eugenicist texts, it must have made for some uncomfortable moments when editor Perkins contemplated this passage in the
first chapter of the draft of the novel that was to become *The Great Gatsby*:

> "Civilization's going to pieces," broke out Tom, violently [that's Tom
> Buchanan]. "I've gotten to be a terrible pessimist about things. Have
> you read 'The Rise of the Coloured Empires' by this man, Goddard? …
> Well it's a fine book and everybody ought to read it. The idea is, if we
> don't watch out the white race will be—will be utterly submerged. It's
> all scientific stuff. It's all been proved…. Well, these books are all scien-
> tific…. This fellow has worked out the whole thing. It's up to us who
> are the dominant race to watch out or the other races will have control
> of things … The idea is that we are all Nordics … and we've produced
> all the things that go to make civilization—oh, science and art, and all
> that." (12–13)

While there was an actual eugenicist named Goddard, it seems likely that Fitzgerald has named his character with an amalgam of Grant and Stoddard's names
and the title, "The Rise of the Coloured Empires," is meant to allude to their principal eugenicist texts. That Fitzgerald means for us to take these ideas scornfully
is suggested by several elements in the passage. First, there's Tom's wife Daisy's
dismissive comments about her husband's latest obsession. She interjects ironically that "Tom is getting very profound. He reads deep books with long words
in them" (13). And Nick, our narrator, concludes, "There was something pathet-
ic in his concentration, as if his complacency, more acute than of old, was not
enough to him any more" (13). But perhaps the most skillful indirect expression
of Fitzgerald's disdain for Tom's "ideas" is the way Tom explains that "Nordics
… produced all the things that go to make civilization—oh, science and art, and
all that." It is that revealingly indefinite "and all that" that suggests how vacuous
Tom's thinking is. Perkins helped to bring into print the ideas that Tom mouths,
but he also held Tom in disdain. In a November 1924 letter to Fitzgerald, Perkins

praises Fitzgerald's portrayal of many of the book's characters, whom he finds "marvelously palpable and vital," and he adds, "I would know Tom Buchanan if I met him on the street and would avoid him" (Kuehl and Bryer 83).

But, while Fitzgerald seems scornful of Tom Buchanan's racism, he also indulges in a blatantly stereotypic portrayal of a Jewish character that might have warmed the heart of Grant or Stoddard. Meyer Wolfsheim, he of the cufflinks made of human teeth, the man who had "fixed the World Series back in 1919," had played "with the faith of fifty million people—with the single-mindedness of a burglar blowing a safe" (73); Wolfsheim, "a flat-nosed Jew" according to the novel's narrator Nick Carraway, "with two fine growths of hair which luxuriated in either nostril" (69). It was "a tragic nose" (72) that, presumably unlike a Nordic nose, could "flash ... indignantly" (70). Wolfsheim was based on crime boss Arnold Rothstein, the man who really did fix the 1919 World Series. Fitzgerald's description of Wolfsheim looks only passingly like the physiognomy of the man on whom he is modelled; the novelist here indulges in a cheap stereotype, linking Wolfsheim's presumably Semitic appearance to his moral depravity.

If Wolfsheim were the only Jew in the novel then we might think of this as simply the cruelly casual antisemitism that characterized the age, an expression of Nordic heebie-jeebies. But I concur with two provocative studies of the issue of racial and ethnic negotiation in American life, the historian Matthew Frye Jacobson's *Whiteness of a Different Color: European Immigrants and the Alchemy of Race* and the literary historian Walter Benn Michaels's *Our America: Nativism, Modernism, and Pluralism*. They share the provocative assumption that Gatsby is Jewish, that Jimmie Gatz's name change to Jay Gatsby is not merely an attempt to acquire a more romantic sounding name, but that it repeats a common practice in American assimilation: name change to obscure ethnic origins. Gatz is an unusual name—one is hard-pressed to find genealogical reference to it—but it is closely related phonetically to Goetz, a common surname of German Jews. It also sounds very much like another common Jewish name, Katz. And while there is a vague reference to an unnamed midwestern Lutheran college Gatsby may have attended, and his father organizes a Lutheran funeral for him, it should be noted that many assimilating German Jews adopted a nominal Lutheranism.

If we think of Gatsby as the Jew trying hard to assimilate, then Wolfsheim becomes not only a vile joke, but also a warning: this is how self-assuredly white America looks on an unassimilated Jew. And this is possibly Gatsby's fate if he can't pull off his transformation into what Nick calls "his Platonic conception of himself" (98). Wolfsheim becomes a projection of goyish racist stereotypes.

Fitzgerald establishes Nick Carraway as an implicit foil for the eugenicists as he recalls his father's advice early in the novel to "withhold judgement" of others, which contrasts with the eugenicists' quick and easy stereotyping of others using pseudo-scientific methods and jargon (1). Furthermore, Nick calls attention to the ways he is akin to Gatsby—both the descendants of immigrants:

> My family have been prominent, well-to-do people in this middle-western city for three generations. The Carraways are something of a clan and we have the tradition that we're descended from the Dukes of Buccleuch, but the actual founder of my father's line was my grandfather's brother who came here in fifty-one, hired a substitute to the Civil War and started the hardware business that my father carries on today. (3)

Nick gently tweaks his family's claim to be of Protestant aristocracy, the Scottish Dukes of Buccleuch, and implies that his ancestors were, in fact, Potato Famine Irish refugees come over in 1851, in the midst of the famine—immigrants reviled by nativists in their own time as much as immigrants from Southern and Eastern Europe are in his. Moreover, in his elegant summation to the Gatsby story, Nick, about to head back to his native Midwest, contemplates how this patch of land he has inhabited for a time, this Long Island, must have seemed to the first Dutch explorers to behold it, a place of wonder, but an Eden already begun to be destroyed when they first set foot on it. If, as the eugenicists insisted, the purity of America was being diluted by early-twentieth century immigrants, the novel suggests that those Dutch sailors—good Nordics all—were the first despoilers of America.

Fitzgerald's portrait of Meyer Wolfsheim, along with another brief racist portrayal of two Black men, justly makes us feel uncomfortable, but, while engaging in a racist stereotype, Fitzgerald at least seems to recognize it for what it is. Moreso, he offers a critique of such thinking at a time when eugenicist ideas held sway with much of educated and comfortable America—apparently even with Fitzgerald's eminent literary editor, Maxwell Perkins.

None of these works make any reference to the anti-immigration legislations of the early 1920s. In fact, the issue of immigration is never addressed in the novels. None of the principal characters are immigrants, unless you were to consider the American and British ex-pats of Hemingway's novel as potential immigrants—to France or Spain. Even if one does, there is no suggestion of an equivalency in the way they are treated in Paris and Pamplona and the ways recent immigrants—Eastern European Jews, Italian Catholics, Greek Orthodox Christians, and others—were regarded in the United States. But the same eugenic drumbeating that led to the Emergency Quota Act of 1921 and the Johnson-Reed Immigration Act of 1924 may have influenced these three important writers to create significant Jewish characters and to examine racial stereotypes associated with Jews with an intense attention they had not brought earlier in their careers, nor were they to bring later. Nick says of Tom Buchanan, "His complacency ... was not enough to him any more." America in the first decades of the twentieth century had changed so dramatically and so quickly that the old complacencies about who we are and what it means to be an American were "not enough ... any more." And so, we embraced paranoid pseudo-science. And so we enacted draconian immigration laws. And so we slammed shut the doors of Ellis Island. And yet our best writers could not prevent the outsiders from occupying the pages of their novels, sometimes as distasteful jokes, sometimes as complicated new realities with which we must grapple, and sometimes as compelling examples of our dynamic and changing culture.

Elizabethtown College

Works Cited and Consulted

Cather, Willa. *O Pioneers!* Vintage Classics, 1992.

———. *The Professor's House.* 1925. Alfred A. Knopf, 1959.

———. "Scandal." *The Century Illustrated Monthly Magazine*, vol. 98, Aug. 1919, pp. 433–45. *Willa Cather Archive*, cather.unl.edu/writings/shortfiction/ss055.

Coates, Ta-Nehisi. *Between the World and Me.* Spiegel & Grau, 2015.

Daiker, Donald. "'One of the Filthiest Books of the Year': Hemingway's *The Sun Also Rises* as Banned Book." Banned in the Heartland, a special issue of *Midwestern Miscellany*, edited by John Rohrkemper, vol. 52, no. 1–2, spring-fall 2024, pp. 39–49.

Faulkner, William. *The Sound and the Fury: The Corrected Text.* Vintage International, 1984.

Fitzgerald, F. Scott. *The Great Gatsby.* 1925. The Author's Edition. Scribner, 2018.

Frazier, Ian. "Old Hatreds." *The New Yorker*, 26 Aug. 2019, as "When W. E. B. Du Bois Made a Laughingstock of a White Supremacist." www.newyorker.com/magazine/2019/08/26/when-w-e-b-du-bois-made-a-laughingstock-of-a-white-supremacist.

Gidley, M. "Notes on F. Scott Fitzgerald and the Passing of the Great Race." *Journal of American Studies*, vol. 7, no. 2, August 1973, pp. 171–81.

Grant, Madison. *The Conquest of a Continent; Or, The Expansion of Races in America.* Charles Scribner's Sons, 1933.

———. *The Passing of the Great Race; Or, The Racial Basis of European History,* 1st ed., Charles Scribner's Sons, 1916.

Hemingway, Ernest. *The Sun Also Rises.* Edited by Michael Thurston, Norton Critical Edition, W. W. Norton, 2022.

Jacobson, Matthew Frye. *Whiteness of a Different Color: European Immigrants and the Alchemy of Race.* Harvard UP, 1998.

Kuehl, John and Jackson R. Bryer, editors. *Dear Scott / Dear Max: The F. Scott Fitzgerald - Maxwell Perkins Correspondence.* Charles Scribner's Sons, 1971.

Kühl, Stefan. *The Nazi Connection: Eugenics, American Racism and German National Socialism*. Oxford UP, 1994.

Marcus, Lisa. "Willa Cather and the Geography of Jewishness." *The Cambridge Companion to Willa Cather*, edited by Marilee Lindemann, Cambridge UP, 2005, pp. 66–85.

Michaels, Walter Benn. *Our America: Nativism, Modernism, and Pluralism*. Duke UP, 1999.

Morgan, Edmund S. *Benjamin Franklin*. Yale UP, 2003.

Okrent, Daniel. *The Guarded Gate: Bigotry, Eugenics and the Law That Kept Two Generations of Jews, Italians, and Other European Immigrants Out of America*. Scribner, 2019.

Regal, Brian. "Madison Grant, Maxwell Perkins, and Eugenics Publishing at Scribner's." *The Princeton University Library Chronicle*, vol. 65, no. 2, winter 2004, pp. 317–42.

Stoddard, Lothrop. *The Rising Tide of Color Against White World-Supremacy*. Charles Scribner's Sons, 1920.

Svoboda, Frederic Joseph. *Hemingway & The Sun Also Rises: The Crafting of a Style*. UP of Kansas, 1983.

Turlish, Lewis A. "The Rising Tide of Color: A Note on the Historicism of *The Great Gatsby*." *American Literature*, vol. 43, no. 3, Nov. 1971, pp. 442–44.

Woodress, James. *Willa Cather: A Literary Life*. U of Nebraska P, 1987.

Yudell, Michael. *Race Unmasked: Biology and Race in the Twentieth Century*. Columbia UP, 2014.

"THAT'S MY MIDDLE WEST"
Nick Carraway's "Reflective" Nostalgia
and Fitzgerald's *The Great Gatsby* at
One Hundred

David Buehrer

The release of the Cambridge Centennial Edition of F. Scott Fitzgerald's *The Great Gatsby* in early 2025 (the novel was first published by Scribner's on April 10, 1925) would seem to necessitate a fresh look at some of the social, cultural, and historical contexts that underlie this iconic American modernist work. Specifically, this essay will examine the intersection of class and place as it impacts many of the novel's characters, particularly considering narrator Nick Carraway's attitudes toward his midwestern origins as they come into conflict with life on Long Island's Gold Coast during the infamous Roaring Twenties. Nick, as he reminisces about what he calls "my Middle West" toward the story's close, seems to embody what Russian essayist and cultural critic Svetlana Boym terms, in her 2001 book *The Future of Nostalgia*, the "reflective" nostalgia of the émigré—one who may dream of or even mourn for the past, but also does not really want it back either, perhaps because he recognizes that "the [old] home[stead] is in ruins," or, as a minimum, has "been ... renovated ... beyond recognition" (Boym 50). This stance contrasts with Jay Gatsby, of course, who as a "restorative nostalgic" believes he can "repeat the past" (Fitzgerald 112),[1] or at least, as a myth-maker, "rebuild the [fictional] lost home" that he comes to take for the "truth" (Boym 41). Nick's "Middle Western city," presumably Minneapolis, does not offer him (much like Fitzgerald from the Summit Hill district in St. Paul), despite his "well-to-do" (Fitzgerald 9) upbringing there, the kind of romantic illusions that for Gatsby become "commensurate to his capacity for wonder" (Fitzgerald 182). As such, Nick concludes that he and those other "Westerners," including Daisy and Jordan from Louisville and Tom Buchanan from Chicago, "perhaps ... possessed some deficiency in common which made [them] subtly unadaptable to Eastern life" (Fitzgerald 178). It is that level of "deficiency," born of class and place in, as Nick sees them, "the bored, sprawling, swollen towns [and cities] beyond the Ohio" (Fitzgerald 178), this paper will critique while bearing in mind Fitzgerald's own revelation of the past, present, and uncertain future that he offers up in his "great" American novel.

As John F. Lavelle and Debbie Lelekis contend, "[t]here is little doubt that anyone who reads *The Great Gatsby* is confronted with it being predominantly concerned with class" (144), evidenced with the book's focus on several "low-class, socially ascendant protagonists" (Nemmers 137), most notably Jay Gatsby but also Myrtle Wilson in her affair with Tom Buchanan. Yet class consciousness for Nick Carraway at any rate is very much tied up with place and the "privileged ideology" (Lavelle and Lelekis 141) that leads him to admit, given his upper-middle-class rearing, that "a sense of the fundamental decencies is parceled out unequally at birth" (Fitzgerald 8), a principle he adopts as a young man from his conservative midwestern father. Nick tells us his great uncle "came here in fifty-one, sent a substitute to the Civil War, and started the wholesale hardware business that my father carries on today" (9). So while Nick's family were not wealthy aristocrats, they were, not unlike the Hemingways of Oak Park, Illinois, "solidly middle-class, ... not rich but landed or to be exact, well-ensconced in the middle-class gentry of [their] community, ... whose views on work and morality were shaped by religion and the belief that" (Lavelle and Lelekis 141), as one biographer puts it, "material success was the just reward for their virtuous private lives" (Dearborn 11). Such "decency" and "reserve" (Fitzgerald 7), that stereotype of what Carol Bly calls midwestern "restraint" (qtd. in Christman 180), seem endemic to Nick's sense of place, with both nature and nurture shaping his character and sense of self. This perspective becomes clear in his reflections on "honesty" and his desire to return to the Midwest, or to a "world ... in uniform and at a sort of moral attention forever," following his "riotous excursions" with Gatsby in "the East" (Fitzgerald 8) during the spring and summer of 1922.

Still, it could be argued that such a nostalgic mythology has always pervaded the literature of the Midwest. As Mark Athitakis maintains in his slim 2016 volume *The New Midwest*, even more contemporary midwestern writers remain "nostalgic for the past" as they "often lament what's been lost in the present" (9), and that is surely Fitzgerald's viewpoint as channeled through the narrative voice of Nick Carraway in *The Great Gatsby*. But even in early-twentieth-century literary works, "The Midwest was [presented as] persistently rural—or, if not rural, indelibly marked by rural values" such as self-reliance and industriousness. This picture of the region became "perfect ... for decades of nostalgic pining for a Midwest that never really existed" (Athitakis 13), therefore—a "mythology" of the Midwest that Fitzgerald, the St. Paul, Minnesota, exile, began to challenge in his fiction. That contestation is principally seen via Nick's reminiscences both early and late in *Gatsby*, at the same time that the writer also seems to "acknowledge[ ] the optimistic pull of the cliché of [m]idwestern values" (Athitakis 14) within the book. Critic Letha Audhuy has made an analogous claim: "In *Gatsby*, there is a moral progression implied by Nick's rejection of the East and return home to the West, which presumably is not a wasteland" (51). However, Nick as "moral exemplar" in the end and the East as "immoral" (Audhuy 54) may well be one of these pernicious stereotypes or clichés about the Midwest and its attendant ideals that Fitzgerald's novel ultimately questions.

But Nick's story of first leaving the Midwest and heading east is part of a larger pattern of movement or migration at the time. As Carraway relates in the opening frame, "I graduated from New Haven in 1915, ... and a little later I participated in that delayed Teutonic migration known as the Great War. I enjoyed the counter-raid so thoroughly that I came back restless. Instead of being the warm center of the world, the Middle West now seemed like the ragged edge of the universe—so I decided to go East and learn the bond business.... permanently, I thought, in the spring of twenty-two" (Fitzgerald 9). That perception of the Midwest as "the ragged edge of the universe" was likely the effect of a spiritual and emotional exhaustion brought on in the war's aftermath: Hemingway felt it, too, as expressed in the story "Soldier's Home" from his first collection *In Our Time*, also published in 1925. Thus, what became that "postwar mood of expatriation" for writers like Fitzgerald and Hemingway "was [actually] a revolt against small-mindedness, Puritanism, provincialism, prohibition" (Brad-bury 35), traits that were regarded as woven into the Midwest's very cultural fabric. For Nick (and for Gatsby and Fitzgerald himself), this entailed a reverse-translation effect—i.e., "Go East, Young Man," to quote the title of a Sinclair Lewis story from 1930—that drove them to the East Coast first for college (Nick, like Lewis, to Yale; Fitzgerald to Princeton), then to New York (Scott and Zelda rented a house in Great Neck, Long Island, the less fashionable West Egg of *Gatsby*, in 1922), and finally to France, where Scott finished rewriting and revising the novel on the Riveria during the summer and fall of 1924. That is, "in a reversal of the east-to-west movement and metaphor of the frontier," Fitzgerald, as well as his characters to differing degrees, "regard[ed] America as the old world, Europe as the new" (Callahan 178). John F. Callahan notes that "[m]ost of Fitzgerald's fellow expatriates were provincials. Indeed, like him, many were Midwesterners [Hemingway, Sherwood Anderson, and Kay Boyle come to mind] who, fed-up with so-called American normalcy, fled eastward to France ... in the 1920s" (176). Nonetheless, these expats would also often harken back to the Midwest as a site of nostalgic origins in their writings.

In general, however, such nostalgia towards one's home—of which Gatsby and Nick, both native Midwesterners, seem to have very dissimilar takes in Fitz-gerald's novel—can, as Svetlana Boym explains, assume "two [distinct] kinds [or forms] ... the restorative and the reflective":

> Restorative nostalgia stresses *nostos* [i.e., "return" or "homecoming"] and attempts a transhistorical reconstruction of the lost home. Re-flective nostalgia thrives in *algia* [i.e., "pain" or "sorrow"], the longing itself, and delays the homecoming—wistfully, ironically, desperately. Restorative nostalgia does not think of itself as nostalgia, but rather as truth and tradition. Reflective nostalgia dwells on the ambivalences of human longing and belonging and does not shy away from the contra-dictions of modernity. Restorative nostalgia protects the absolute truth, while reflective nostalgia calls it into doubt. (Boym xviii)

By these definitions, the restorative nostalgic is decidedly romantic, the reflective nostalgic modernist in mindset or belief. This also marks an essential difference between Jay Gatsby and Nick Carraway and their respective points of view in *The Great Gatsby*, especially considering the "emotional topography of memory" (Boym 52) each character evokes. As Boym further elucidates, "[m]odern nostalgia is a mourning for the impossibility of mythical return, for a loss of an enchanted world with clear borders and values" (8). This sense of mourning or loss is plainly Nick's position on the Midwest by the end of his story, or "in the wake of [Gatsby's] dreams that temporarily closed out [Nick's] interest in the abortive sorrows and short-winded elations of men" (Fitzgerald 9), as he puts it.

This frame novel closes, consequently, as it began, with Nick's musings on returning "back home" to the Midwest, "[a]fter Gatsby's death [and with] the East [...] haunted for [him]" (Fitzgerald 178), but now from the perspective of both physical and temporal displacement. In Chapter 9, Nick recalls "vivid memories" of "coming back West from prep school and later from college at Christmas time" (177), of "the Chicago, Milwaukee and St. Paul railroad" that he took and from its train car looked out on the "real snow" and "dim lights of small Wisconsin stations, [with] the sharp wild brace" of the winter night's air making him and his fellow west-bound travelers "unutterably aware of our identity with this country for one strange hour, before we melted indistinguishably into it again" (Fitzgerald 177). This in turn sets up Nick's most exacting description of his former home:

> That's my Middle West—not the wheat or the prairies or the lost Swede towns, but the thrilling returning trains *of my youth*, and the street lamps and sleigh bells in the frosty dark and the shadows of holly wreaths thrown by lighted windows on the snow. I am a part of that, a little solemn with the feel of those long winters, a little complacent from growing up in the Carraway house in a city where dwellings are still called through decades by a family's name. I see now that this has been a story

of the West, after all—Tom and Gatsby, Daisy and Jordan and I, were all

Westerners.… (Fitzgerald 178, emphasis added)

The piece would appear to be autobiographical, as these "reflections [were] written in St.-Raphael, France, [in 1924] about [Fitzgerald's own] 1921 return [train trip] to St. Paul, Minn." (Kenner 37). But while Nick's Midwest may be biographically consistent with Fitzgerald's, it is also what Boym would call a "false homecoming" that the narrator imagines because it is very much in the past (or "of [his] youth," as he phrases it), which past he, as a reflective nostalgic, recognizes is "irrevocab[le]" (Boym 49)—even while Gatsby does not. That failed vision constitutes, in short, the tragic flaw leading to this title character's downfall and near-mythological "Death by Water" (Audhuy 53) in the book's penultimate chapter.

Given this temporal context, therefore, it appears inaccurate to claim, as critic Owen Cantrell does, that "Carraway views his Midwest through rose-colored glasses" (51), or that "[a]t the end of the novel, Nick retreats to the Midwest, but his Midwest is often a stereotypical landscape, more of a pastoral fantasy than a lived reality" (Cantrell 53). Such a reading fails to account for the above passage's obvious placement of Nick's outlook as representing the distant past, a dream of his "youth," as opposed to his current jaded attitude toward those "positive" (Cantrell 59), if stereotypical, "midwestern moral values" (Zhang 134) like "honest[y]" and "honor" (Fitzgerald 179), as is exhibited in his parting conversation with Jordan Baker. Or, as Ronald Berman reminds us in his 2017 book *F. Scott Fitzgerald and the American Scene*, "When Nick ends the story, he remarks that he isn't 'provincial' anymore. That is to say the values he starts out with are ineffective against the way things are [now]" (72). Here, the Midwest does not offer Nick "an avenue of escape" (Cantrell 54) so much as a place to land for his mere acquiescence to or acceptance of "the way things are." As a reflective nostalgic, Nick is a realist in his sensibility, not a romantic idealist invested in some sort of "pastoral fantasy" of his home region. Boym argues that such "reflective nostalgia cherishes shattered fragments[2] of memory and temporalizes space"; in addition, it "does not pretend to rebuild the mythical place called home[, since] it is enamored of distance, not of the referent itself" (Boym 49, 50). I agree, because for the reflective nostalgic, like Nick at the end of *The Great Gatsby*, lament for past memories, and not a futile attempt to somehow restore that past, is what matters. As Boym summarizes, "[r]eflective nostalgia is a form of deep mourning that performs a labor of grief both through pondering pain and through play [i.e., irony] that points to the future" (55).

Such a viewpoint is in contradistinction to the book's eponymous hero as a "restorative" nostalgic, since "only false memories can be totally recalled" (Boym 54), and with Jay Gatsby this rings especially true. Perhaps it is significant, then, that Gatsby's restorative nostalgia has him returning, literally and figuratively, to Louisville, more the Upper South[3] than Midwest, in an effort to recreate a mythical past with Daisy, who remains altogether cynical about her "white girlhood" (Fitzgerald 25) there, as she quips to Nick and Jordan in Chapter 1. Daisy appears fashioned after Fitzgerald's own "golden girl," Zelda Sayre, "the headstrong belle of Montgomery, Ala.," whom he married in 1920 (Kenner 34). And, as Scott Donaldson suggests in his article "Scott Fitzgerald's Romance with the South," "It is the Southern girl in whom Fitzgerald invests his romantic illusions—and it is by the Southern girl, too, that these illusions are shattered" (6). That said, neither Nick nor Gatsby, "the North Dakota parvenu with mysterious sources of wealth"—and, by extension, Fitzgerald, "[the] Minnesota parvenu" (Kenner 42) raised in middle-class St. Paul—has any inclinations of romance associated with that Upper Midwest from which they hail. Thus, when Gatsby returns from France following the Armistice, he uses "the last of his army pay" not to go to his childhood home, but instead "ma[kes] a miserable but irresistible journey to Louisville," and finds himself "revisiting" all of "the out-of-the-way places to which [he and Daisy] had driven in her white car" (Fitzgerald 155), still very much in search of the illusory dream of their short-term love affair. Gatsby's nostalgic "return" or rather "pilgrimage to Louisville" (Donaldson, "Possessions" 205) is doomed to disappointment from the start, therefore. Ultimately, Gatsby's restorative nostalgia has him isolated from the present, distanced from the past he wishes to regain, and dislocated from the future he will never see, existing in a no-man's-land from which his only escape is through death. And Gatsby's delusionary plan—that once Daisy is "free" of Tom, "they were to go back to Louisville and be married from her house—just as if it were five years ago" (Fitzgerald 111)—again reveals a nostalgic vision completely divorced from reality. Maybe, too, Gatsby's Louisville represents his own "Lost Cause," or the creation of a historical myth in place of what is empirically true. In his book *Hemingway vs. Fitzgerald: The Rise and Fall of a Literary Friendship* (1999), Scott Donaldson also offers a biographical source for Gatsby's conviction: Scott "was brought up Catholic, … and his father, a failure in business, was a romantic Southerner [from Maryland], who taught his only son to embrace the lost cause of the South" (217).

In truth, Gatsby does not acknowledge his actual rural midwestern place of origins at all, nor the father who still lives there, which again indicates his lack of nostalgia for the area. Mr. Henry C. Gatz "arrived from a town in Minnesota" (Fitzgerald 169) where Gatsby had bought him a house two years before (174). However, it is three days after his son's death before he even finds out about it when he "saw it in the Chicago newspaper.... It was all in the Chicago newspaper" (169), and only then "started [East] right away" (169). But there will be no "homecoming," or burial, in the Midwest, since even his father acknowledges the son's desire for this final geographical displacement. When Nick asks Mr. Gatz if he wants "to take the body West," the old man "shook his head. 'Jimmy always liked it better down East. He rose up to his position in the East'" (Fitzgerald 170). Still, his father associates Jimmy's budding "greatness" with another renowned resident of Minnesota, James J. Hill, the self-made man and railroad tycoon whose mansion on Summit Ave. in St. Paul "provided an icon for the American success story" (Bruccoli 22). Mr. Gatz tells Nick, "If he'd [i.e., Jay Gatsby né James Gatz] of lived he'd of been a great man. A man like James J. Hill. He'd of helped build up the country" (170). Here, Gatsby's greatness is thus allied with the material wealth and industry of the West, with those who "built" the country, its physical infrastructure, and not with the country's moral or religious idealism, which no longer counts in characterizing the American Dream. In his 2008 non-fiction book *Dreaming Up America*, novelist Russell Banks makes a comparable argument, contending that one "early form of the American Dream … the New England Puritan dream of God's Protestant utopian City on a Hill," eventually gets supplanted by the capitalistic "City of Gold that Cortez and Pissarro dream of finding" (6). Or, as Sarah Churchwell puts it in her critical introduction to the Cambridge Centennial *Gatsby*, "The shift from spiritualism to mercantilism"—and remember, it is "Dutch sailors" or merchants, not religious Puritans, that Nick envisions spying the "fresh, green breast of the new world" (Fitzgerald 182) at Long Island, New York—"is the whole point: America has lost faith in its spiritual idealism and built a new world that is merely material without being real, because it has lost its capacity for idealism and wonder" (xliii). This "shift" is again noted in Nick's musings in *Gatsby*'s last pages on that "old, unknown world" (182) of America's "irrecoverable romantic past" (Donaldson, "Possessions" 210).

Furthermore, Jay Gatsby is so dismissive of his midwestern roots—he is the child of "shiftless and unsuccessful farm people" from North Dakota, which Nick is only "told" about "very much later" (Fitzgerald 103)—that when asked by Nick early on about "what part of the Middle West" his invented family of "wealthy people … all dead now" (67) supposedly comes from, Gatsby replies, "San Franscico" (68). His origin story is itself fantastic and includes the then-teen James Gatz "beating his way along the south shore of Lake Superior" (100) until he meets Dan Cody, the rich Western prospector whose yacht becomes the vehicle to get him out of and away from that "some nobody" (Fitzgerald 69) from no place condition. So, the "enormously wealthy" (12) Tom Buchanan of Chicago, or more precisely Lake Forest, "Chicago's most socially prominent suburb" (Donaldson, *Hemingway* 31), is astute in lambasting Gatsby as "Mr. Nobody from Nowhere" (132) who has the temerity to have a "presumptuous little flirtation" (Fitzgerald 137) with his wife Daisy. Donaldson concurs with this appraisal: "In a sense, Tom is right to characterize Gatsby in this way, for he lacks any mentionable social background," and Gatsby's many gaudy possessions "represent his attempt to establish himself as Somebody, or at least not Nobody" ("Possessions" 207). Tom's hailing from Lake Forest is also biographically meaningful, since this is the same hometown of Ginevra King, Scott Fitzgerald's first love, "the seventeen-year-old ... who would one day be the principal model for Daisy Buchanan in *The Great Gatsby*" (West 50). Ginevra definitely matched what became Fitzgerald's "dreams of the perfect girl: beautiful, rich, socially secure, and sought after" (Bruccoli 54). While their two-year, mostly epistolary relationship ended in January 1917 when she jilted Scott for the wealthy and more socially connected William Mitchell, whom she would go on to marry in September 1918, "Ginevra [nevertheless] gave him [Fitzgerald] access, early on, to a world of money and privilege that he might not otherwise have observed" (West 106). In the end, however, for Scott with Ginevra[4] as for Gatsby with Daisy, "[s]he came from a more exalted social universe, one he could visit but not belong to" (Donaldson, "Possessions" 198)—and hence the futility of his, like Gatsby's, "passionate quest for an unattainable ideal" (Donaldson, *Hemingway* 36).

In his 2017 essay "On Being Mid-Western: The Burden of Normality," Phil Christman maintains that the "paradox" of "the Midwest is a particular place that ... thinks of itself as an anyplace or no-place" (173). Similarly, nostalgia for the Midwest, as mirrored by Nick Carraway's perception of it in *The Great Gatsby*, might be said to be equally mixed or paradoxical. Moreover, Christman's claim that "our reckoning with the Midwest is perpetually arriving, perpetually deferred" (175) seems close to that delayed homecoming which Svetlana Boym, in her book *The Future of Nostalgia*, attributes specifically to the reflective nostalgic. In short, Nick's "Middle West" may also expose the "double consciousness" he, and his creator, F. Scott Fitzgerald,[5] has of the place: "the Midwest as an America not yet achieved; the Midwest as an America soaked in the same old American sins" (Christman 183). And one hundred years on, Fitzgerald's *The Great Gatsby* still speaks cogently to the class inequities in American society, as well as offering an assessment of region both paradoxical and cliché-ridden. "That's my Middle West," Nick tells us—it may well be ours, too, that "anywhere, and also nowhere" (Christman 178) some of us choose to call home.

Valdosta State University

Notes

1. Unless otherwise indicated, all page references to the novel, cited parenthetically by author, are to the Cambridge Centennial Edition of *The Great Gatsby*, edited by James L. W. West III with an introduction by Sarah Churchwell, Cambridge UP, 2025.

2. Fragmentation of characterization and setting is integral to Fitzgerald's modernist narrative technique in *Gatsby*. Nick conveys a similar sensibility following his talk with Gatsby about the past love affair the latter had with Daisy: "Through all [Gatsby] said, even through his appalling sentimentality, I was reminded of something—an elusive rhythm, a *fragment* of lost words, that I had heard somewhere a long time ago.... But ... what I had almost remembered was uncommunicable forever" (Fitzgerald 113, emphasis added).

3. See Berman's *F. Scott Fitzgerald and the American Scene* (2017) for a fuller portrayal of Louisville, which "was known for great houses, for great wealth" (9), "although [it] was famously the most northern of the cities of the South and entirely conscious of northern industrial values" (11). In addition, its "social life ... was haute bourgeoisie and did not imitate the plantocracy of the deep South.... It was never a backwater or lost place in history and remains one of the great exhibits of the Gilded Age," a "city ... notably practiced in the religion of success" (60). Louisville thus best epitomizes that "distance between social classes" (Berman 60) depicted in the novel, as with the image of "indiscernible barbed wire between" (Fitzgerald 150) the young Jay Gatsby and Daisy Fay.

4. In his 2006 book *The Perfect Hour*, James L. W. West III describes the enormous class divide separating Ginevra from Scott:

> [Fitzgerald] was not on firm ground in Lake Forest. He was of Irish
> descent and was a Roman Catholic, both of which were disadvan-
> tages there. Most of the boys in Ginevra's social set were backed by
> high social status and family money. Their fathers were railroad ex-
> ecutives or lumber barons or department-store magnates or prom-
> inent physicians, attorneys, or judges. [Ginevra's father, Charles
> King, was a successful banker who, like Tom Buchanan, was rich
> enough to "own [a] string of polo ponies" on his estate (West 5)].
> Scott's father was a wholesale grocery salesman, and not an espe-
> cially successful one. Scott did have good looks, charm, and literary
> ability, but these were not the trump cards. His visits to Lake For-
> est must have been difficult for him…. [H]e was a young man of
> modest means, hobnobbing with the rich. (West 42)

It was at one of those "difficult" visits to Lake Forest, in August 1916, that
Ginevra's father is purported to have said, within Scott's hearing, that "poor
boys shouldn't think of marrying rich girls" (qtd. in Donaldson, *Hemingway*
35), a sentence which would prove to be the death knell for the young lovers' relationship, but was also perhaps the spur for Fitzgerald's future literary
representations and achievements.

5. In *Hemingway vs. Fitzgerald* (1999), Donaldson comments upon the im-
    portant role Edmund "Bunny" Wilson's March 1922 untitled review essay
    for the *Bookman* (reprinted in *The Shores of Light*, 1952, pp. 27–35) had
    on first establishing the young novelist's literary reputation, for better and
    worse: "The emphasis throughout was on what Fitzgerald lacked. In con-
    sidering the writer himself, Wilson stressed Fitzgerald's Irish and middle-
    western origins. These had left him without qualities that he ought to have
    had" (279), such as "a sound basis of culture and taste" and "values … of a
    firm foundation" (qtd. in Donaldson, *Hemingway* 279). It could well be such
    presumed "deficienc[ies]" (Fitzgerald 178) that the author, through his nar-
    rator Nick, alludes to ironically in the closing pages of the novel, especially

in light of the "double consciousness" toward place and class origins that Fitzgerald would seem to embrace.

Works Cited and Consulted

Athitakis, Mark. *The New Midwest: A Guide to Contemporary Fiction of the Great Lakes, Great Plains, and Rust Belt.* Belt, 2016.

Audhuy, Letha. "The *Waste Land* Myth and Symbols in *The Great Gatsby.*" *Etudes Anglaises*, vol. 33, no. 1, 1980, pp. 41–54.

Banks, Russell. *Dreaming Up America.* Seven Stories P, 2008.

Berman, Ronald. *F. Scott Fitzgerald and the American Scene.* U of Alabama P, 2017.

Boym, Svetlana. *The Future of Nostalgia.* Basic Books, 2001.

Bradbury, Malcolm. *The Expatriate Tradition in American Literature.* BAAS, 1982.

Bruccoli, Matthew J. *Some Sort of Epic Grandeur: The Life of F. Scott Fitzgerald.* 2nd rev. ed., U of South Carolina P, 2002.

Callahan, John F. "'France Was a Land': F. Scott Fitzgerald's Expatriate Theme in *Tender Is the Night.*" *French Connections: Hemingway and Fitzgerald Abroad*, edited by J. Gerald Kennedy and Jackson R. Bryer, St. Martin's P, 1998, pp. 173–86.

Cantrell, Owen. "'It's Not Polite to Talk About Yourself': Regional Identity and Erasure in the Midwest from F. Scott Fitzgerald to *Mad Men.*" *MidAmerica*, vol. 41, 2014, pp. 39–61.

Christman, Phil. "On Being Mid-Western: The Burden of Normality." *Red State Blues: Stories from Midwestern Life on the Left*, edited and introduction by Martha Bayne, Belt, 2018, pp. 171–86.

Churchwell, Sarah. Introduction. Fitzgerald, pp. xiii–xliii.

Dearborn, Mary V. *Ernest Hemingway: A Biography.* Knopf, 2017.

Donaldson, Scott. *Hemingway vs. Fitzgerald: The Rise and Fall of a Literary Friendship.* Overlook P, 1999.

———. "Possessions in *The Great Gatsby.*" *The Southern Review*, vol. 37, no. 2, 2001, pp. 187–210.

———. "Scott Fitzgerald's Romance with the South." *The Southern Literary Journal*, vol. 5, no. 2, spring 1973, pp. 3–17.

Fitzgerald, F. Scott. *The Great Gatsby*. 1925. Edited by James L. W. West III, Cambridge Centennial Edition, Cambridge UP, 2025.

Kenner, Hugh. *A Homemade World: The American Modernist Writers*. Johns Hopkins UP, 1975.

Lavelle, John F., and Debbie Lelekis. "The Sun Also Rises for Some: Hemingway's Exploration of the Ideologies of Social Class in *The Sun Also Rises*." Lavelle and Lelekis, eds., pp. 141–56.

———, editors. *The Working Class in American Literature: Essays in Blue Collar Identity*. McFarland, 2021.

Nemmers, Adam. "'One had to have castes': Class, Culture, and Ideology in *An American Tragedy*." Lavelle and Lelekis, eds., pp. 121–40.

West III, James L. W. *The Perfect Hour: The Romance of F. Scott Fitzgerald and Ginevra King, His First Love*. Penguin Random, 2006.

Wilson, Edmund. *The Shores of Light: A Literary Chronicle of the Twenties and Thirties*. Farrar, 1952.

Zhang, Aiping. *Enchanted Places: The Use of Setting in F. Scott Fitzgerald's Fiction*. Greenwood P, 1997.

FLOYD DELL'S OPTIMISM, FEMINISM, AND RADICAL REJECTION OF SEXUAL THRALLDOM

Marilyn Judith Atlas

Floyd Dell—a midwestern editor, reviewer, critic, novelist, and playwright—was a major force during several decades of American modernism and played a significant part in the political and social movements of the 1910s and 1920s, first as editor of Chicago's *Friday Literary Review,* a supplement of the *Chicago Evening Post,* and then as editor of *The Masses* and co-editor with Crystal and Max Eastman of *The Liberator.* Dell's art is both social satire and psychological study demonstrating in a variety of ways his interest in the right to choose—for both men and women—and in the survival of artists and artistic integrity. In his two 1925 novels, *This Mad Ideal* and *Runaway,* human integrity is first about loyalty to one's dreams and individual talent, and only afterwards about love, marriage, children, responsibility to others, and community. Dell's work challenges contained, ordered, conservative thinking, and his main characters often prefer, at least for a time, the messy chaos of the untried, dangerous, and new. In both of his 1925 novels, avoiding forced conformity drives the plot. Dell's main characters, mother and daughter Nan (Gloriana) and Judith Valentine, and father and daughter Michael and Amber Shenstone, contemplate and explore the rich possibilities of the open road—whether married or single: better a short life with creativity and integrity than a long one where art and agency are second-class citizens is their basic philosophy. The behavior and motives of these characters are often misunderstood by their families and communities, but each character is determined to follow his or her own insights and impulses as he or she figures out whether to marry or whether to remain married, and each suffers real-world consequences but also gains self-respect. In both novels Floyd Dell explores the plight of American turn-of-the-century artists—middle-class, white, heterosexual modernists—rejecting the mores of the genteel tradition, trying for something more feminist, hopeful, and honest, rejecting the judgment of communities that are afraid of freedom and difference. These heroes marry their dreams, and not always one another. For each of these characters—even Amber, who in *Runaway* chooses a bohemian community-sanctioned marriage to a poet/lawyer—having agency trumps sexual thralldom, a state of being enslaved or in bondage and without volition.

Floyd Dell, a feminist and modernist, studies the real according to his lights and in these two novels avoids the type of romance that leaves men and women without choice and agency. Main characters, men and women, do not have to die if they make a wrong choice or find traditional marriage or family life overly oppressive and interfering with their ability to be actualized human beings. They are allowed to err and even to recover and thrive. Beginning the journey is portrayed as being worth the consequences. These novels do not end with marriage as the only goal of adulthood: only healthy, brave individuals help create thriving, kind communities, and Dell explores not only what thwarts individuals, but what diminishes communities. In these two novels, Dell is being radical and feminist and in the second one, *Runaway*, also comic; men can, and sometimes do, choose art and self over love, and so do women, and in the case of Amber Shenstone and George Willoughby, can have both. Conservative small towns such as Nebo, Pompton, and Beaumont need to change, or need to be left behind, and individuals can and do make new, controversial, and liberated choices. Dell, in his fiction, is writing beyond the ending of the "marriage plot" found in such novels as Charlotte Brontë's *Jane Eyre* (1847), and Edith Wharton's *The House of Mirth* (1905) and *Age of Innocence* (1920). He takes on the ridiculousness of censorship in *This Mad Ideal* and perverse organizations like the KKK in *Runaway*. In 1925, the values of America were changing and women as well as men, in these novels, are depicted as questioning authority and claiming their birthright to be creative, productive individuals. Sexuality, in these novels, is portrayed as a part of life, but not a part that leaves all characters, men and women, choiceless and trapped. Ahead of his times in many ways, Dell is careful to demonstrate that women as well as men can have artistic dreams and talents, and he often rewards them for their bravery and determination.

Dell's first novel, *Moon-Calf*, published in 1920 when he was 33 years old, was a bestseller, focusing, like Sinclair Lewis's *Main Street*, on complicated, and too often, hypocritical, small-town Midwest life. After *Moon-Calf*, where Felix Fay is the main character, he published *The Briary-Bush* (1921), an extension of *Moon-Calf* in which Felix Fay, also this novel's main character, decides to leave his small town and go to Chicago, pursue his craft, and feed his intellectual hunger. Dell's fourth novel, *Janet March* (1923), is a study of the break-up of the patriarchal family, and centers on a woman, Janet March, who practices more personal and sexual freedom than her culture allows. Neither *The Briary-Bush* nor *Janet March* were as successful as his first novel, *Moon-Calf*, and *Janet March* became a center of political controversy: the censors argued that it is immoral. There is an abortion in the novel: Janet March, the novel's hero, dares to be sexual out of wedlock and, without shame, gets pregnant and ends her pregnancy without telling her lover: her body, her choice. In his 1971 Twayne study of Floyd Dell's biography and literary career, John E. Hart explains that to avoid censorship Floyd Dell and Knopf, the novel's publisher, agreed to suppress the novel and the book was withdrawn from sale in New York and Massachusetts bookstores (Hart 93).

Undeterred by the censors' responses to the serious feminist questions of women's bodily autonomy and their right to choose, in 1925 Dell published two additional novels that also deal with women's bodily autonomy, sexuality, creativity, and marriage: *This Mad Ideal* and *Runaway*. While these two novels examine sexual choices, sexual thralldom, marriage, and family, Dell compromised: neither novel explores taboo issues, such as abortion rights, that caused him problems earlier with censors.

But these two 1925 novels are radical: men and women who marry and find marriage is oppressive for them, even if they have children, are allowed to leave their marriages and attempt to find a way back to a healthy, more authentic self without the author condemning them. Like Susan Glaspell's radical and experimental play *The Verge* (1921), these two novels interrogate the institution of marriage, and how it is impossibly oppressive for some, as well as the meaning of love and the role of sexuality in human relationships, particularly as it pertains to artists, both male and female. Unlike Glaspell's *The Verge*, which ends in tragedy and madness for the main character, Clare, these two novels make rejecting or leaving lovers or marriages worth the journey, and characters do not regret their decisions to be non-normative, nor do they go mad and become murderers. Whether the characters' goals are achieved, or even, in the case of Jud and Nan Valentine, whether they survive, Dell's main characters understand their own motives and are happy to have taken their chance. The main characters of these two novels, Judith Valentine in *This Mad Ideal* and Michael Shenstone and his daughter Amber in *Runaway*, choose art and self over sexual thralldom, middle-class comforts, and community approval and support, although sometimes they get these, and there is no tragedy. The main characters risk death, but no character, male or female, implodes trying to negotiate a world of science or creativity, even when mistakes are made. Taking chances is honorable and rewarded in *This Mad Ideal* and *Runaway*.

Some books are marketed to succeed: during World War II the US military distributed over 150,000 copies of the 1925 novel *The Great Gatsby* to American servicemen, helping to posthumously revive the reputation of its author F. Scott Fitzgerald, who died in 1940 (Scott). If there were no paperbacks, if the novel was not distributed in this way, would it be so front and center to our understanding of classic midwestern, or American, or world fiction? These two novels by Floyd Dell did not receive this type of marketing, so contemporary readers might not have heard of them, but like *The Great Gatsby*, they offer important insights into the meaning of healthy marital love and into the psychology of creative outsiders who choose their own, sometimes not very traditional, ways. These 1925 Dell novels are fine, entertaining, and well-written. They posit that leaving home can be essential and returning home is sometimes possible. In sum, 1925 was an amazing year for works written by midwestern writers: F. Scott Fitzgerald published *The Great Gatsby*, Willa Cather *The Professor's House*, Ernest Hemingway

In Our Time, Theodore Dreiser *An American Tragedy,* Langston Hughes *The Weary Blues,* and T. S. Eliot "The Hollow Men." Dell's two 1925 novels, *This Mad Ideal* and *Runaway,* are important, well-written additions to this list and deserve a great deal more attention than they are receiving.

Neither of these two Dell novels takes place in the Midwest, but Dell is a major midwestern writer, and though he chose to place his characters outside of the Midwest for these two novels, he still used his midwestern experiences—geographical and social—in creating them. Born in 1887 in Barry, Illinois, Dell moved to Quincy, Illinois, in 1889, and to Davenport, Iowa, in 1903. In 1908 he relocated to Chicago, Illinois, helping to create the Chicago Renaissance before settling in Greenwich Village. In these novels, characters dedicated to their art and/or hunger for something other than marriage are willing to sacrifice a great deal—including love relationships, sexuality, marriage, and children—in order to have the chance to pursue their dreams and/or develop their craft. The small-town life, even the small-town experience of community in Chicago's Roger's Park and Fifty-seventh Street district during the Chicago Renaissance, informed Dell's frustration with and interest in the survival of creative individuals within conservative communities—whether real midwestern communities or fictional ones in New England (Nebo and Pompton) or in some geographically undetermined American space (Beaumont).

What interested Dell, just like what interested Fitzgerald, was human "selfishness," but Dell's selfishness was the selfishness of the self-aware individual who knows that to give up on one's dreams or one's art for the sake of love, stability, even a community's respect, cannot be the road to happiness or to fostering healthy communities. Individual integrity and art come first in Floyd Dell's novels, not for art's sake, but for the individual's or the artist's soul's sake. Experimental prose does not interest Floyd Dell, but exploring modern survival in an age of cultural change and negotiating one's way through judgmental, misguided, misinformed, narrow communities that are quick to condemn humans, censor art, cull library stacks for the sake of "morality," and end up fostering perverse societies such as the KKK do.

In the first of these two 1925 novels, *This Mad Ideal*, Dell creates a character—a reader, dreamer, and poet—Judith Valentine, who sees marriage as a trap. Judith, distressed, trying to figure out what to do about her relationship with Roy Sopwith, reminds herself that marriage is dangerous: "They had found out that marriage was the end of everything. And they wanted to go on" (*This Mad Ideal* 167). The young Judith explains to Roy, the young artist she loves, that she is willing to give up love, marriage, and children to pursue poetry, and he too confesses to her that he wants to be an artist more than anything else in the world, but he quickly discovers he does not, or at best he is ambivalent about choosing art first (*This Mad Ideal* 167). Their commitment to their art is far from identical, just as their upbringing is very different from each other's. Judith's mother, Nan (called "Gloriana" by her family), has lived separately from her father, Jud Valentine, and Jud is encouraged by her to do what he requires, to leave the family and Nebo, and to pursue his dream of being an important reporter. Jud goes to Boston, becomes sick with consumption, and dies, but his dream of becoming famous or his choice to leave his family are never belittled by the narrator, Judith, or Nan. Judith's mother understands and encourages her husband's choice, and she also leaves Nebo when she has the opportunity to pursue her art, to sing and act with a travelling group, and while she also dies trying to fulfill her dream of being a performer, her death is also never belittled by the narrator. In these Dell novels, taking one's chance is good and natural for both men and women. Like her parents, Judith Valentine, poet, chooses art over love and a conservative, safe lifestyle. The third-person narrator explains and accepts her choice helping the reader understand why she chooses art over love and why she feels she cannot have both, given who she loves and the context of her, and her lover's, fragility.

When readers first meet Judith Valentine, she is 4 years old, living out on a gully in a two-room house with her mother, happy enough and free. A bit later in the novel we see her as an independent child collecting eggs, selling them, making pennies with which to buy candy and importantly old magazines. Even as a very young child, hearing and reading stories are her passion. Her mother,

Nan, a woman who longs for the stage, is her playmate. Judith, until she is 11, is raised by a single mother on folk songs, fairy tales, poetry, and the dream of freedom. Nan loves her absent husband, Jud, and explains to her daughter that she sent him to Boston willingly: without being able to work on his craft, Jud, in Nebo, is miserable and broken (*This Mad Ideal* 21). Nan allows her daughter to believe that Jud will return when he has found his success and regardless, "maybe we shan't wait for him. We'll start in to become famous ourselves before very long.... we'll have our chance, too. And when it comes, we'll take it!" (*This Mad Ideal* 21). When Nan's chance arrives, she does take it, secretly disappearing from Nebo: Nan and daughter travel with a small vaudeville group, and for a short time Nan has an outlet for her craft, but she too succumbs to illness and Judith is orphaned. On the road, Daddy Kiernan, once a Latin professor, the troupe's head, teaches Judith mythology and Latin, and she embraces the value of honoring priceless and essential dreams. "Hours of Beauty, go slowly, slowly!" she learns from Daddy Kiernan (29). Beauty, one's craft, and/or freedom are worth everything to Nan, Jud, and now Judith.

When her mother dies, Judith is sent to her mother's sister, Emma, to live in conservative Pompton, also, like Nebo, no promised land. But she remembers that dreaming, craft, and freedom have been honored in her original, primary family, and she takes this knowledge and the myths, songs, fairy tales, and poetry with her to oppressive Pompton. Particularly, she takes with her the "Walk Along Song" that she and her mother used to sing together, a two-person song in which marriage is refused:

O madam, I will give to you
The keys of Canterbury,
And all the bells of London
Shall ring to make us merry,
If you will be my joy,
my sweet and only dear,
And take a walk with me, anywhere!

and its answer,

> I shall not, sir, accept of you
> The keys to Canterbury,
> Nor all the bells of London
> Shall ring to make us merry.
> I will not be your joy,
> Your sweet and only dear,
> Nor take a walk with you anywhere! (*This Mad Ideal* 15)

Marriage is dangerous; refusing it is perfectly acceptable, and Judith sings and remembers the second part of this song throughout the novel as consistently as she is able.

This Mad Ideal repeatedly sets up situations where the traditional choices are not the best ones for its characters. Viewpoints matter, are fluid, but are not to be completely trusted. Characters and readers can learn from history, or the Bible, or the names of places, or elders, but must be careful to remember that history does not identically repeat itself and that elders and well-intentioned people can be misguided.

Names of places matter in this novel, but what happens to Moses on Nebo might not happen to Judith Valentine in Nebo. Nebo, the mountain from which Moses sees the promised land, a land he, because of his sins, will never be allowed to enter, is a metaphor for imperfection and partial failure. So far no one from the Valentine family has entered a promised land either, but that does not make such entrance impossible. Judith's next stop, provincial Pompton ("pompous") is also not that promised land, but that does not mean New York cannot be that promised land for her.

In this novel, children need protection, but they also need dreams and self-respect. Well-meaning high school principal Mr. Sopwith lectures on the ethics and wisdom of censorship, but has not a clue as to what is valuable and what is not. He attempts to convince the school's students that it is sometimes best not to read classics such as Thomas Hardy's *Jude the Obscure*. Principal Sopwith does much harm to his children, Madge and Roy, and to independent students like Tennessee Franklin and her freethinking father, and ultimately to his community, because these characters are unable to thrive in the oppressive and controlling atmosphere Sopwith fosters (*This Mad Ideal* 79). And there is plenty of irony to go round: Nebo can be the mountain from which a girl like Judith Valentine sees the promised land, for her, New York; and the principal of Pompton's high school, by encouraging censorship and unwittingly fostering resistance, can help create the poet and brave woman that Judith becomes.

In Pompton, Judith is taught to be ashamed of her mother, who is seen as a moral degenerate, and of her father, who is labeled a family deserter; in Pompton she is taught to forget everything she learned from her mother. To her uncle, aunt, and cousins, Judith seems wayward like her mother. But Judith does not learn everything she is taught. Instead, she learns to take what she needs and think for herself. Judith is beautiful and charming, and being part of this conservative family is a dragon that Judith learns, metaphorically, to slay, so she can inherit the kingdom of New York. In Pompton she experiences bullying and shame, but she prevails as a reader and poet, thinking through her experiences, forming her own perspectives and values, and gathering her strength so she can escape and become the poet and person that she wishes, and needs, to be.

As soon as she arrives in Pompton, at her mother's funeral, she falls in the snow, damaging her back, and for a long time quietly suffers before a doctor, Dr. Hugh, treats and strengthens her back—an extensive and painful process—teaching Judith that with the right guidance healing is possible. Judith treasures this doctor and her ability to move freely once again. When the people of Pompton condemn him for falling in love with a married woman, Judith does not. She is only sorry that he must lose his Pompton practice and the community.

She learns that Dr. Hugh's gift to her is priceless but that some gifts come with too high a price tag. Principal Sopwith offers to get her a scholarship to Bridgewater College, where he will soon be teaching and where she will have beauty and integrity defined for her. Principal Sopwith believes he is giving Judith a chance; her aunt, uncle, and cousins also see this scholarship as a wonderful opportunity, but Judith sees it as entrapment and honors her own point of view above all others. When her opinion differs from those around her, she sticks to her own perspective. For instance, she finds sexual attraction and love with her misguided principal's son, Roy, who, at first, wishes to be a fellow artist, a fellow traveler and friend, and to sacrifice for art just like her, but his context and motivation are very different from Judith's and this love cannot be sustained. Roy's father is oppressive and important to the community of Pompton, and Roy does not need to leave Pompton or to create art as much as he needs, like his older sister, Madge, to get out from under his father's control. Although Roy draws and paints beautifully, and would like to be an artist, what he wants even more is independence from his father, respect, community, acceptance, and marital happiness with Judith: earning a living painting houses will do for him—he need not study painting—if he can wed Judith Valentine. This is not what Judith needs and wants, however. She cannot fulfill her own dream and Roy's, and she chooses her own.

Judith's relationship to sex is complicated. First, she is made to feel ashamed of her body. She is not allowed to be a tomboy (*This Mad Ideal* 47); her cousin Elsie causes her to think of the sexual act as something disgusting (*This Mad Ideal* 48–49), and after her first kiss with Roy she immediately becomes afraid of the ramifications: "'Why did I let him kiss me?' she demanded angrily of herself" (*This Mad Ideal* 122). She needs friends and space to become who she needs to be, and she sees sexuality as potentially getting in the way of these dreams. Judith's goal is to have a full and creative life, to see what she can do. Regardless of the punishments she receives, Judith will not, and cannot, choose to be like other people, and instead chooses to at least try to be happy and creative according to her own nature. She refuses to be entrapped by sexuality or love and will not choose either over her art.

Judith is not always brave, but she wishes to be. Earlier in the novel Tennessee Franklin, the daughter of a freethinker and mechanic, fights Principal Sopwith overtly—and loses. Judith is too afraid and shy to tell Tennessee how proud she is of her for standing up to Principal Sopwith and how sorry she is that it has cost Tennessee so much—ostracism (*This Mad Ideal* 92–93). But because she so admires Tennessee, Judith writes a prize-winning poem about Joan of Arc, "Joan Before Her Judges," honoring Tennessee. It is published first in the school paper and then in the community paper. Unfortunately, but expectedly, the poem is generally misunderstood. When the poem's beginning lines get scrambled in the school paper, Judith, for a short period, rejects the poem, but then, after receiving Roy's praise, Judith rereads her poem and also decides it is good. It is then that Judith resolves to pursue the craft of writing poetry in her future (*This Mad Ideal* 106). Judith and Roy authentically love each other, but being together, marriage, is the wrong choice for her. She explains to him,

> I couldn't understand about my mother and father separating, when I was little; but I do now. It wasn't that they didn't love each other. That was what puzzled everybody so—they *did* love each other. And it was because they loved each other that they had to do what they did. They had found out that marriage was the end of everything. And they wanted to go on. (*This Mad Ideal* 121, italics in original)

Roy attempts to understand why marriage is not possible for him and Judith and agrees to give up the idea of marriage and go to art school, but sex and insecurity get in the way of their friendship (*This Mad Ideal* 122), at least for Roy. Roy falls in and out of understanding what Judith is trying for and the sacrifices both will have to make to achieve their artistic goals. He does what she requires, but what he recurrently wants is Judith more than his art, and this is a problem for Judith.

This Mad Ideal does not end with love and marriage, nor does it end with death or madness. Roy tries art school in New York, leaves town while Judith works for the town newspaper saving money for her future venture into the art world, but emotionally Roy cannot handle his separation from her. His sister, Madge, believes Roy has had a nervous breakdown because of Judith, and when Judith comes to Boston to try and figure out what is wrong and why she has not heard from Roy, Madge gives her the ultimatum of marrying Roy or leaving him alone. Judith Valentine chooses her dream; she chooses New York.

Madge is also a rebel who runs away to avoid her father's attempted micro-management of her soul, but when Judith comes to Boston to see Roy, Madge, who works for a Boston paper, at first refuses to understand Judith's behavior toward her brother. Roy remembers and forgets the terms of their alliance and friendship, and the forgetting causes him hardship.

He begins to fear Judith is having an affair. When Judith befriends another man, Hugo Massinger, a newspaper reporter to whom she rents Roy's Pompton shack, a shack he purchases hoping to become independent from his father, hoping to perhaps share it for a time with Judith after they wed, Roy crumbles. Hugo Massinger and Judith do become close friends, but Hugo does not replace Roy in any way for Judith, yet Roy, insecure because although away from Pompton he hears that Hugo and Judith are spending time together, both during the day and at night, loses faith in Judith's commitment to their love. The community of Pompton also does not understand Judith's engagement to one man who is away and the substantial amount of time she spends with another man, and they label her promiscuous and condemn her. No one understands Judith's values or strength, and she, because of non-normative behavior and unfair gossip, loses her valuable and prized job at the Pompton town newspaper. Judith is innocent. She no more wants to marry Hugo than she wants to marry Roy, and when Hugo shows interest in marrying her, she recommends that he marry another woman whom he has been seeing. Although Hugo does become engaged to this other woman, Judith is not perceived by the Pompton community as an unselfish and practical woman. She does not belong with someone like Hugo, a narcissistic, if charming, vagabond and knows it. Although Hugo's engagement causes others to erroneously conclude that Judith is a jilted woman, a victim of her bad behavior, choices, and values, the reader knows that she has encouraged Hugo's engagement and is relieved by it. Naïve and innocent, Judith is surprised by the community's condemnation of her, but she is strong and proves her resilience, even when the scandal's fallout causes her to be fired from her newspaper job.

Worried by Roy's recent silence she leaves for Boston. Arriving at Madge's home, where Roy is recovering from what seems to be a nervous breakdown, she explains herself as best she can to Madge, a "new woman," a newspaper woman, Roy's once bohemian and runaway sister who should, and ultimately does, understand:

> "I'm going away," said Judith.
>
> "Back to Pompton?"
>
> "I think I shall go to New York. My things are at the station."
>
> "New York?"
>
> "Yes. I have a little money to live on for a while. I'll see what I can do."
>
> Neither of them spoke of Roy.
>
> "Well—good luck, Judith."
>
> Madge bent and kissed her, and Judith tiptoed out of the apartment.
>
> In her berth that night, troubled with doubts and flushed with eagerness, Gloriana's daughter tossed wakefully, waiting for the new day. (*This Mad Ideal* 246)

Judith's mother had wanted a chance to be creative, to be whole, and is strong enough to let her husband leave her and pursue his dreams. Judith is also that strong: with Roy she would not be an artist; neither would Roy. In her mind, if they love one another, they cannot be together. Judith Valentine has inherited the legacy of taking chances, of allowing and leaving loved ones to be, or to attempt to be, who they need to be, without guilt or shame. One must begin the journey, and continue it, if one is ever to reach the promised land.

Earlier in the novel, Judith, as a 14-year-old girl, is beaten by her well-meaning uncle for standing naked on her head on a rock that jutted out into the sea. She is defined as "savage" because of her behavior, but she is not savage (*This Mad Ideal* 54); rather, she is just an enthusiastic, free-spirited, and budding artist, a lover of poetry, who forgets other people and that private settings can become public—quickly. William Wordsworth's 1807 poem "The World Is Too Much with Us" makes Judith feel a certain way and dramatically reciting the poem naked on the beach, standing on her head, gesturing, gives her pleasure. Caught in the act of being the star of her own dream, she is severely condemned and punished, but shame and humiliation do not stick to this young girl's sense of herself. Judith's dreams are deeper than her cousins' bullying and weaker than her uncle's barrelstave [sic]. Belittled and shamed by her uncle for being nude on the beach, she remains unrepentant and unbroken.

No one owns Judith Valentine. At the end of the novel, she is 21, with just a little inherited money from her aunt, Phoebe, who condemns Judith's and Judith's mother's freedom yet still keeps her great niece in her will and ironically bequeaths to her the financial means to take her chance. Her aunt, a representative of Nebo, serves as the unlikely enabler of Judith's journey to her own mount Nebo: because of this small inheritance, Judith can at least for a while realistically fantasize about her promised land of New York keeping her dream alive until she can actually get there. Judith is not Moses, and she has not sinned, so her entrance to the promised land, unlike Moses's, is permissible. It is not guaranteed, but it is possible, that Judith Valentine will be able to not only enter her sacred, creative space, where poetry, dreams, and ideals lead the way, but even be able to thrive there.

In *Runaway*, later that same year, Dell creates a novel, just as serious but more comic, about a husband and father, Michael Shenstone, who cannot be pinned down by marriage or financial success and who runs away from a marriage with the beautiful, potentially wealthy and kind Helena Boyce. Michael, a reporter and vagabond, deserts his wife and 5-year-old daughter, Amber, in search of himself, and maybe art. He is attracted to China, Marco Polo, and poetry, and though a father and a successful enough businessman, he is deeply unhappy in Beaumont. He leaves his town, his home with Helena and Amber, and returns to the country cottage on Vandover Lane where he and Helena made their first Beaumont home. But his need for "elsewhere" is very strong, and when Helena goes to a relative's funeral, he deserts the family and heads for China. He is gone for seventeen years. When he returns, Helena is no longer alive and Amber is 22 years old—a beauty who dangles several men and, with a free spirit and fortune of her own, creates quite a bit of commotion. Amber thinks she needs a man to help her escape Beaumont. Michael, reunited with his daughter, proves that he cares for her and has not returned to Beaumont to simply collect his dower, one-third of Helena's substantial estate. He also proves that while he is a less than serious artist, he is nevertheless a serious man who after seventeen years believes it is time to reunite, or at least try to reunite, with his daughter whom he misses. He plans to spend a month in Beaumont and during that time he is able to help his daughter as well as win back the town's approval.

Floyd Dell explores, but does not condemn, Michael Shenstone. Dell, in a serious and by turns very funny novel, demonstrates that one can run away from home, be a vagabond, a half-serious writer, a family deserter, and still return home and do good for one's family, neighbors, and oneself, that one can desert a daughter and still find a way to help her to achieve her dreams—marry a poet/lawyer/mentee/friend, George Willoughby—and even possibly become the actual writer of the scholarly work "The Travels of Marco Polo" or perhaps the autobiography "The Travels of Michael Shenstone."

Michael's behavior, rather than destroying Amber because he deserts her, helps to liberate her. She is free to choose what she needs because her father models that behavior. Male or female, in these two Dell novels, it is okay for humans to dream, be different, be single, or be married. Again, sexual thralldom is rejected, and authentic love is not controlling. In *Runaway*, unlike in *This Mad Ideal*, lasting, strong, healing marriage is possible. Happiness, Dell seems to be suggesting, can be achieved in an imperfect world—and money helps.

Like in *This Mad Ideal*, beauty must be defined by individuals and in *Runaway* a broken jade dragon becomes a symbol of ferocity, companionship, and acceptance, bringing anxiety, but also comfort and solace. Running away can be good and right as well as cruel—and fluid, complex viewpoints, forgiveness, a sense of humor, self-awareness, and a bit of luck are all essential to a good outcome.

The little jade dragon, an ancient symbol of the impossible and vain longings that have through all the ages tormented and allured the human soul, by the end of the novel is broken by Michael and then successfully glued together, becoming a symbol of modernism's conversation, attraction, and interrogation of a deeper, more scientific form of realism: "break-up" (Kuh 7–15). The dragon, once to be feared, becomes a friend after Amber and her now husband, George Willoughby, begin their journey together and Michael Shenstone finds himself in his original cottage, with his repaired dragon, more contented than he has ever been. Nothing is permanent and not everything is tragic—Michael is now accepted in Beaumont, where he has serendipitously helped break up the power of the KKK just by being in Beaumont and legal heir to one-third of Helena's estate, although he does not want the money, and his daughter does not need it. Comfortable, appreciated, reunited with his now happy daughter who has chosen her present path, Michael considers staying in Beaumont at his charming cottage for a while. At first, he had come only for a month, but now he feels that this is a natural, beautiful, and kind home where he might be able to actually write his Marco Polo book. At the end of the novel, the runaway father of a 5-year-old daughter and husband of a beautiful, kind wife, is not punished, but rewarded for doing his best and being authentic, caring, and kind. Michael need not wander forever, and he has found acceptance, and even some companionship, with an art object that he originally perceived as hostile:

> The little jade dragon looked over him drowsily. The gleam of sunset light on its miniature curves and coils of cold hard half-translucent stone caught and held his dreaming gaze. An image older than the conscious memory of the race. The image of something beautiful and terrible,—outside of man's sane hopes, yet inexorably a part of man's destiny,—sometimes darkly hostile and sometimes inscrutably consoling. An enigma like himself. (*Runaway* 303–04)

Michael Shenstone, the runaway, has found his way back to a comfortable, although not simple, self and a comfortable home where he can feel respected and empowered and create what is in him to create.

Every once in a while, a writer, male or female, opts in his or her writings to counter the "sexual thralldom" implicit in conventional romance plots. His or her characters choose not to marry or choose to leave marriages, and their author makes the radical decision not to punish or belittle them because they are doing the best they can according to their lights. These radical writers, Dell among them, refuse to create frameworks that elide or absorb difference; rather, authors like Dell honor difference and unsettle cultural values and norms, honoring what should have been honored all along: self-actualization. In 1925, Dell chooses to construct narratives that redefine and reconstruct social respectability, and he denies seductive patterns of feeling that are culturally mandated, policed, and monetized. Instead, he creates narratives that break acceptable sequences, undoing the structures incorporated into mainstream discursive practices. Floyd Dell is a radical disruptor of conventional romance plots because he allows men and women to demonstrate that choosing oneself is viable, ethical, and worthy, and if one makes errors, some at least, can be corrected.

These two novels, one centering on a female character and one on a male character, encourage readers to consider inclusiveness rather than punishment and judgment of complex, creative characters who find traditional marriages wrong for them. In 1921 Susan Glaspell explores radical female choice in her experimental and radical play *The Verge*; in 1925 Floyd Dell honors his friend and colleague by writing two novels that continue her exploration of difference ending his not with tragedy, not with the central female character imploding, but with an acceptance of difference: thriving and radical choices can and do hold hands in both of these 1925 novels. Dell is writing beyond the ending (DuPlessis 1–20) of the marriage plot. Marriage is not good for everyone and it is certainly not an "ending," and through these novels, Dell demonstrates that figuring this out as best one can is good enough.

While Dell's perspective and ideas concerning marriage and loyalty to one's art and nature are radical for his time, as is his refusal to create tragedy for those characters who are not governed by traditional values, Dell's artistic form is traditional. In 1925 marital values are changing and these works help readers see some of the ways marriage is and ought to be interrogated. In an earlier work, *Women as World Builders: Studies in Modern Feminism* (1913), Dell attempts to define the feminist movement and explore women such as Charlotte Perkins Gilman, Emmeline Pankhurst, Jane Addams, Olive Schreiner, Isadora Duncan, Beatrice Webb, Emma Goldman, Margaret Dreier Robins, Ellen Key, and Dora Marsden, explaining what feminism means to him, through his particular male lens, and them, and how these women exemplify various pieces of women's freedom. Modern feminists rightfully cringe at some of Dell's now old-fashioned, essentialist theories, and his entitlement as a man to categorize and define these flesh-and-blood women might be seen as less than ideal, but the book is important because it allows readers to understand his evolving sensibility as artist and feminist, a person who told Margaret Anderson at the beginning of her career when he hired her as a book reviewer for *The Friday Literary Review* to always consider her standpoint and her values when writing reviews: "In heaven's name don't tell the story of the book! Bring to bear upon the book, in aesthetic terms, your attitude toward life" (Baggett 44). Anderson, in her creation of *The Little Review*, seemed to have taken Dell's guidance to heart. But Dell also follows his own advice: what interests him about feminism, socialism, and Freud are how these theories affect his own life, and in 1925 he works out some of his questions about marriage and its relationship to personal integrity and art, attempting through his novels to understand how both men and women are harmed—and helped—in the case of Amber—by this institution.

Dell's world is not the world of post–World War I angst. T. S. Eliot begins his experimental, brilliant, and powerful 1925 poem "The Hollow Men" powerfully evoking and interrogating despair:

> We are the hollow men
> We are the stuffed men
> Leaning together
> Headpiece filled with straw. Alas!
> Our dried voices, when

We whisper together
Are quiet and meaningless
As wind in dry grass
Or rats' feet over broken glass
In our dry cellar

Shape without form, shade without colour.
Paralysed [sic] force, gesture without motion; (Eliot)

There is no "shape without form" in either of Floyd Dell's 1925 novels; rather, there is a radical optimism that the world which must be changed to allow for authentic life, will be changed.

Before World War I, American modernism seems to embrace the idea that progress is possible and that taking a close look at the world, breaking it up and reassembling it, will help humans improve it, and in 1937 we have evidence that fascism is marching, and cannot be stopped. But in 1925, when these two novels are published, Floyd Dell indicates that good, creative, life-giving choices are perhaps unlikely, yet absolutely possible. Dell creates characters such as Judith Valentine and Michael and Amber Shenstone and examines who they are and how they might thrive—even in a troubled world.

Langston Hughes in *The Weary Blues* also offers his 1925 readers exciting new language and form exploring characters and underrepresented and invisible communities and through poetry making them palpable. Here is a bit of the poem named "The Weary Blues," experimental, powerful, essential, first published in 1924 in the journal *Opportunity*, and a year later published by Knopf in a book of Hughes's poetry:

Droning a drowsy syncopated tune,
Rocking back and forth to a mellow croon,
    I heard a negro play.
Down on Lenox Avenue the other night

By the pale dull pallor of an old gas light

 He did a lazy sway....

 He did a lazy sway.... (Hughes 5)

The poem is musical and powerful; the musician and the first-person narrator are both unforgettable. In this poem, Hughes uses dialect and allows minority voices to be heard; his last five lines rhythmically capture the inner beauty and torture of a man experimentally and uniquely telling an American story that needed, and needs, to be told.

 All these works capture something about 1925 and human difference. Floyd Dell's novels should matter to those interested in psychological studies of men and women responding to loneliness, opportunity, and compulsory marriage. Near the end of Dell's autobiography, *Homecoming*, he writes about his novels,

> It would be a period of cynicism—already it was, under President Harding, a period of tolerance for the grossest corruption. The era was unfavorable for me as a novelist, I felt; this accidental popularity of mine would not endure.... I would write the kind of novels I wanted to write, and the public could take them or leave them; ... I would write in fictional terms the true story of the break-up of the old patriarchal family in contemporary America. (360–62)

Here are some of the events marking global lives in 1925: *Ben-Hur*, a fictional story about Christ and revenge is being played in theaters; the Nazi SS is being founded; John Simon Guggenheim offers his first fellowship; Benito Mussolini declares himself dictator of Italy; the Scopes Monkey Trial in Tennessee forces the nation to consider Darwin's theory of evolution and whether it should be taught in schools; and Nellie Tayloe Ross becomes the first woman governor in the United States (Wyoming). Clearly America in 1925 is frightened, complex, and contradictory, and American artists like Floyd Dell are grappling with some of the world's confusion and roar. The Roaring Twenties are perhaps forcing the moment to its crisis—class, race, racism, gender, inequality, science, and religion are not being ignored. In 1925, like in 2025, humans are unsure, confused, and going forward—regardless.

And Floyd Dell is a part of that roar. Only 38 years old in 1925 he attempts to unravel the complexity of what it means to be fully human for women and for men. By 1925 he is the father of two boys and married to his second wife, Berta Marie Gage. If radicalism is extremism, he is not extreme, but if it can contain the idea of being rooted, nuanced, and willing to disrupt the normative conventions of family and marriage—he is indeed radical. This part he has figured out: sexual thralldom is destructive, a state of being enslaved or in bondage, of helplessness and having one's choices taken away, and that, he depicts in these two novels, can never be good for men or women. In romance novels, heroines often experience this state, but not in *This Mad Ideal* or *Runaway*. Love and marriage are very important in both novels, but not more important than freedom to choose and rechoose if one has made the wrong choice. There is much to admire in this young and evolving midwestern writer who is radical in his exploration of break-up: how fictional families function for characters who need and choose to at least attempt to be fully human, the subject and agents of their one precious lives.

Ohio University

Works Cited and Consulted

Anderson, Margaret. *My Thirty Years' War: The Autobiography.* 1930. Horizon Press, 1969.

Atlas, Marilyn Judith. "Harriet Monroe, Margaret Anderson, and the Spirit of the Chicago Renaissance." *Midwestern Miscellany*, vol. 9, 1981, pp. 43–53.

Baggett, Holly A. *Making No Compromise: Margaret Anderson, Jane Heap, and The Little Review.* Northern Illinois UP, 2023.

Butler, Francelia. "Parnassus in the 1920s: Floyd Dell Contemplates His Own Period." *Tennessee Studies in Literature*, vol. 12, edited by Richard H. Dillard, 1967, pp. 131–48.

Dell, Floyd. *Homecoming: An Autobiography.* Farrar and Rinehart, 1933.

———. *Love in Greenwich Village.* 1926. Ayer, 1970.

———. *Runaway.* George H. Doran Company, 1925.

———. *This Mad Ideal.* Alfred A. Knopf, 1925.

———. *Women as World Builders: Studies in Modern Feminism.* Forbes and Company, 1913.

DuPlessis, Rachel Blau. *Writing Beyond the Ending: Narrative Strategies of Twentieth-Century Women Writers.* Indiana UP, 1985.

Eliot, T. S. "The Hollow Men." *Poems: 1909–1925,* Faber & Faber Limited, 1925. poets.org/poem/hollow-men.

Glaspell, Susan. "The Verge." 1921. *Plays—Complete Edition,* Monee, 2022, pp. 28–97.

Hart, John E. *Floyd Dell.* Twayne, 1971.

Hite, Molly. Review of *Writing Beyond the Ending: Narrative Strategies of Twentieth-Century Women Writers* by Rachel Blau DuPlessis. *SubStance, Contemporary Italian Thought,* vol. 16, no. 2, issue 53, 1987, pp. 80–81.

Hughes, Langston. "The Weary Blues." 1925; 1926. *The Weary Blues,* Knopf, 2021.

Kuh, Katharine. *Break-up: The Core of Modern Art.* New York Graphic Society, 1965.

Miller, Nancy K. *The Heroine's Text: Readings in the French and English Novel, 1722–1782.* Columbia UP, 1980.

Noe, Marcia. *Three Midwestern Playwrights: How Floyd Dell, George Cram Cook, and Susan Glaspell Transformed American Theatre.* Indiana UP, 2022.

Range, Peter Ross. *1924: The Year That Made Hitler.* Little, Brown, 2016.

Scott, A. O. "It's Gatsby's World, We Just Live in It." *The New York Times,* 27 Mar. 2025. www.nytimes.com/interactive/2025/03/27/books/great-gatsby-100.html.

Tanselle, G. Thomas. "Sinclair Lewis and Floyd Dell: Two Views of the Midwest." *Twentieth Century Literature,* vol. 9, no. 4, Jan. 1964, pp. 175–84.

Walters, Thomas N. "Literary Radical: The Apple Pie Evolution." *Pembroke Magazine,* no. 11, 1979, pp. 194–205.

"THERE'S SOMETHING IN IT THAT GETS HOLD OF A MAN"
Two Michigan Farm Novels of 1925

Robert Beasecker

Of the eight novels classified as midwestern farm fiction that were published in 1925, two are set in Michigan. G. D. Eaton's *Backfurrow* appeared in February and *Green Bush* by John T. Frederick some seven months later, in September. The authors of these two novels, G. D. (Godfrey Dell) Eaton and John T. Frederick, also have several points of similarity: they were born within a year of each other, and both had first-hand farming experience, were university graduates, and embarked on literary careers. At the time of their publication, no reviewer made any connection or comparison between the two novels, and as neither was recognized as a literary classic, both faded from public notice after a few months in the marketplace. As will be seen, it would take another forty years before the critical juxtaposition of *Backfurrow* and *Green Bush* would yield some interesting insights about these novels and the genre in general.

A rough-and-ready list of the varied characteristics of the farm novel can be summarized thusly: "Some renderings are idyllic and nostalgic, reflecting the positive value and reward of hard work on bountiful family farmsteads; others are grim accounts of unremitting labor that comes to naught through the vicissitudes of weather, health, or commodity prices" ("Farm Literature" 237). *Backfurrow* and *Green Bush* make use of some of these attributes and also possess many similarities. For example, their young male protagonists, Ralph Dutton and Frank Thompson, close to being the same age, come to farming in different ways but experience many of the sorrows and joys that working the soil can deliver. In the first decades of the twentieth century, they are neophytes in the ways of the world and have naïve, romantic, and confused love/lust views of women. They respond to the siren call of the attractions of the "big city"—in both these novels that city is Detroit—that in the end turn out to be only illusions. They also have adult mentors who are physicians, pharmacists, and fellow farmers who offer much wise advice that sometimes is taken, sometimes not. Both see education as desirable: Ralph's basic learning was attained from the local district schools, but Frank has an undergraduate degree from the University of Michigan and continues graduate studies. They both exhibit jealousy and resentment when their respective wives assume farming activities, finances, and management of their farms when their husbands become ill or otherwise incapacitated. How Ralph and Frank ultimately handle their lives in agriculture comprises different sides of the same rural coin.

G. D. Eaton[1] was born in Plymouth, Michigan, in 1894, and was the eldest of four siblings. His father, an advertising executive for the J. L. Hudson Company in Detroit, was killed in a pedestrian-truck accident in 1912. Eaton's mother soon remarried, and he spent a few summers working on his stepfather's farm in western Oakland County, where he gathered firsthand experience that would provide the agricultural background for *Backfurrow*. By 1917 he was the office manager for a small Detroit company, and he served in the medical corps of the US Army during World War I. After the war he went to Ann Arbor, where he matriculated in 1919 at the University of Michigan, from which he received the AB degree in 1923. While at the university he became notorious for his forceful letters to the *Michigan Daily*, the campus newspaper, inveighing against complacency. His candid ideas put him at odds with the university administration while the student body either admired him or hated him as a radical. He served as the literary editor for the school newspaper in the summers of 1922 and 1923. By 1927 he had relocated to New York City, where he worked for the Associated Press and was the founder and editor of the monthly opinion journal *Plain Talk*, somewhat modeled on H. L. Mencken's periodical *The American Mercury*. Eaton died in June 1930 at the age of 35 after a short illness that resulted in paralysis and heart failure. He is buried in Detroit with his parents, and on his gravestone is proclaimed, "Novelist, Journalist, Book Critic, Linguist, Founder of "Plain Talk" ... US Veteran of Foreign Wars." His posthumous novel, *John Drakin*, was published in Milwaukee in 1937 by an unnamed friend, whose unsigned foreword indicates the novel has autobiographical elements and characterizes Eaton as one who was "clean in mind, tolerant of all, save the intolerant, honest and unflinching in his own convictions, and big enough for fight against the injustices and dishonesties inflicted on others" (Foreword, *John Drakin* 9).

John Towner Frederick is better known for his critical essays and other works championing midwestern literature—most notably *The Midland*, the influential journal he founded and edited in 1915 at the age of 22—than he is for his two farm novels (Reigelman 58, 60). Frederick, an only child, was born on his parents' farm near Corning, Iowa, in 1893 (Anderson, "John T(owner) Frederick" 203) and thus became intimately familiar with all aspects of farm life from a very early age. His studies at the University of Iowa were interrupted due to lack of funds, so Frederick taught high school until he could return to complete his degree. Teaching literature at the University of Iowa and subsequently at Notre Dame, where he became chair of the English Department, Frederick also spent considerable time actually farming, both in Iowa and in Michigan, occasionally abandoning the classroom to work the land (Bush 10). In 1919 Frederick purchased 1,600 acres near Glennie, Alcona County, and moved there with his wife and young son and began clearing the land and farming. It is the specific location where his second farm novel, *Green Bush*, is set, and Frederick's descriptions of the soil, the small lakes, the building of a farmhouse, the planting of crops, the weather, and the general atmosphere of that part of northeastern Michigan are what he experienced himself. It is likely the novel was written contemporaneously with the work he was doing with his farm. Over the next forty-plus years Frederick and his family regularly moved among Michigan, the family farm in Iowa, and his teaching duties in Iowa and Notre Dame. Frederick died in 1975 and is buried with his parents, first wife, and one son at Springport Cemetery in Harrisville, Michigan, just a few miles north of the Lake Huron town of Greenbush.

Backfurrow

In February 1925 the venerable New York firm G. P. Putnam's Sons published G. D. Eaton's naturalist novel *Backfurrow*. The publicist and dust jacket blurb writer accurately asserted that the story is "of an individual and his effort to escape from an environment into which he fits but indifferently" (*Backfurrow*, front jacket flap). The individual in question is Ralph Dutton, and the story follows him from his early days into his mid-twenties; interestingly he is the same age as the author Eaton. Ralph is illegitimate; his father is unnamed and his mother leaves Ralph in the hands of her parents to raise on their farm before she leaves the area because of the scandal. The grandparents' fifty-acre farm, ambiguously set somewhere in mid-Michigan—most likely western Oakland County—is a poor one, because of its rocky and hilly soil. Ralph as a youngster helps with chores as best he can, but his aging grandparents are unable to keep up with the work required. The illness and death of his grandmother when Ralph is fifteen deplete the bank account and contribute to Ralph's grandfather's death shortly thereafter. Surprised and dismayed that the farm was not left to him, Ralph is soon thrown off the property by his uncle.

Ralph, having had news of his mother's death some years before, now has no family refuge and he fends for himself by becoming a hired man at a nearby farm. There he works a variety of jobs, carefully saving his money so he can escape the hard labor of agriculture and head for the big city, where he thinks he will find opportunities to better himself financially and improve his education. In the event, he takes the train to Detroit and begins to find work, but always menial jobs at skimpy wages. He delights in the discovery of the public library, where he is able to borrow books that widen his literary horizons. However, a downturn in the economy throws Ralph out of work, and when he cannot find another situation, he bitterly realizes that after six months in Detroit he must return to the only thing he really knows: farm work. Returning to his familiar township he becomes a hired man for a succession of farmers, the son of one remarking on Ralph's slightness of build, "[y]ou ain't no farmer ... you won't never be one" (*Backfurrow* 95). He meets Alice, a beautiful young woman from Detroit who has married a local farmer, and they converse about how much she likes the countryside; about a year later, in the fall of 1914, she has grown depressed and listless and, fed up with farm life, flees back to the city with her child: the idyllic dream of rural living has evaporated. Ralph understands Alice's feelings.

His desire for learning pushed aside by his day-to-day labors, Ralph is reminded of his interest by two men just passing through the area on separate occasions and whom he meets at the local tavern. The first is a salesman and former college professor, dismissed from his position for having a dalliance with the dean's daughter. The second encounter is with a philologist from an eastern college who talks with Ralph about country life and country morality, a conversation that leads Ralph to attempt the seduction of Ellen Tupper, the daughter of a neighbor farmer and only child who does the heavy work for her father and mother. Ellen initially resists Ralph's advances, but ultimately in June 1915 he and Ellen wed. They move to Ellen's farm with her father, a poor fifty-acre spread much like Ralph's grandparents' farm. Much is made of the exhausting work, Ellen's pregnancy, her father's death, their subsequent indebtedness, and hopes for a beneficial harvest. His uncle then offers to sell his grandparents' farm to Ralph, which he accepts, leading to more work and reconfiguration of plantings. He realizes that his hope to again relocate to the city has now vanished and that the improvement of the farm is his prime interest.

In 1917 the United States enters the Great War, and Ralph's farmer neighbor, mentor, and father-figure Herman Schlick is suspected by his neighbors to be an enemy alien; however, Ralph remains a steadfast friend and supports Herman. In the meantime, Ellen has a second child and on Armistice Day, has a third, named Peace, who dies after a short illness in early 1919. The cruelties of Michigan weather send a freeze that wipes out Ralph and Ellen's tender fruit tree plantings, and the general harvest is poor. The watchword of skeptical optimism from them both is "[p]erhaps things would be all right" (*Backfurrow* 288). But, further in debt and with another child due, Ellen appears to Ralph as slovenly, heavy, spiritless, and apathetic. Affection for each other has been lost. The return of Jean Fox, who had left a neighboring farm after eloping with a hired man, inspires Ralph to begin an affair with her, with her encouragement. As he becomes more involved, he plans to leave Ellen and the children and decamp to Detroit with Jean. She rebuffs his assumption and reveals only a passing infatuation for Ralph. The latter, as a result, has a nervous breakdown and needs hospitalization. After a long recovery, Ralph is never the same person and by default allows Ellen to effectively run the farm while he takes care of the children. His scattered thoughts at the end of the novel review fragmentary memories of people in his life, but he is now effectively powerless to renew any of his former hopes and desires.

Green Bush

In September 1925 the decade-old New York publisher Alfred A. Knopf brought out John T. Frederick's novel *Green Bush*. Knopf had also published his 1923 farm novel *Druida*, the story of an intrepid Iowa farm woman that was well-received by critics. For *Green Bush*, Frederick used the locale of his farm in Glennie and the nearby Lake Huron towns of Greenbush (one word here) and Harrisville in northeast Michigan. His protagonist, Frank Thompson, like Ralph Dutton in *Backfurrow*, is an only child. Frank is about 20 and is the son of the editor and publisher of the county newspaper who also enjoys farming a small plot that had been his parents' land. Frank had entered the University of Michigan at sixteen, having had successfully passed advanced courses in high school. Now with a baccalaureate degree, Frank is prepared to return to Ann Arbor to begin graduate studies. During the summer he enjoys helping his father with both the newspaper and the farming; his mother, however, hates the farm, which is a continual bone of contention: "That's always the way with the farm—it comes before the paper or your family or anything else" (*Green Bush* 33). Frank and his father talk about the latter's call to the soil and how much he'd rather do farming and sell the county newspaper, and his father tells Frank, "I expect you'll go on and be a professor like your mother wants you to" (*Green Bush* 38).

Before Frank returns to Ann Arbor, his mother hires Rose, a girl from a farm five miles inland. Because Frank's mother has a chronic illness, Rose helps with housework and cooking. Back at the university, Frank hears that once his master's degree is attained there most likely will be a position for him in the English

Department. Then in November he receives the news that his father has died and he must return to Green Bush. After the burial service Frank thinks about his father and "the impersonal aloofness of the earth, of this little space which he had loved and which had destroyed him" (*Green Bush* 67). Frank's mother suggests he stay home and continue the county paper, at least in the short term, to which Frank agrees.

Frank's stay in Green Bush continues through the winter and into the following spring. On a spring day Frank and Rose walk to his father's farmland, where they discover a social, if not romantic, connection. Frank shares his plans for the farm with his mother, but she tells him that the farm has been listed for sale; disappointed, Frank concentrates on improving the newspaper. Although ostensibly approving of Frank's success, his mother has secretly placed the newspaper for sale, and when a potential buyer arrives unannounced, Frank is angered by his mother's betrayal and realizes it is her way of getting him back to his university studies. He agrees to keep running the newspaper until the new owner takes over, but his relations with his mother become quite cool and distant.

Rose's father comes under suspicion for serious legal transgressions, and he sends her to Detroit to avoid possible trouble at home. When he is later exonerated, Frank travels to Detroit to give Rose the news and to go on to the university to continue his studies. Rose finds work in a Detroit store while Frank is kept busy with school and work in Ann Arbor. After having no contact with his mother for weeks, Frank learns that she had been brought to the university hospital by her Green Bush doctor and has already had an operation, from which she dies a few hours later. After the funeral in Green Bush, he visits Rose in Detroit and tells her about his mother's death. They then get married, and Frank decides to leave the university and return to Detroit with Rose and find work there.

Early in the next year they are dissatisfied with their jobs, rooms, and their mediocre pay. They return to Green Bush to see about his mother's estate. They visit Rose's family and talk about the availability of the neighboring farm and consider their future. Rose asks, "[D]o you think you want to farm, Frank? ... Would you be happy here?" (*Green Bush* 221) and in answer he comes back the next day with the deed. Rose soon discovers she is pregnant. In the fall Frank purchases a stump-puller whose cable fails and deals a serious injury that leaves him an invalid for months. During that time Frank broods on his condition, thinking of university classes and friends, and resents Rose for her strength and ability to take on more of the farm responsibilities. In February, after a heavy ice storm, Rose goes into labor and is having a difficult time; roads are impassable, and telephone lines are down so Frank must take Rose to the hospital in Green Bush by sleigh. After a harrowing trip they arrive safely, the baby delivered and Rose out of danger, but Frank has reinjured himself and he too is in the hospital. The doctor informs Frank that he needs an operation lest he face amputation and possible death.

The operation is a success and when he can return to the farm, a walk through the land refreshes his philosophy of life and death: "Strength flowed into him from the sunlight and soil" (*Green Bush* 277). Soon Frank finds he can gradually do more around the house and farm, but not the heavy work. Later in the summer he learns that the county newspaper is for sale, as is his mother's house. He and Rose decide to keep and work the farm, with Frank spending a few days in Green Bush each week running the paper. The following summer Frank is offered a teaching position at the university, but he responds, "my own life seems to me likely to be richest and fullest here on the land" (*Green Bush* 301).

Critical Reception

Both novels received mixed reviews from newspapers and magazines at the time of their publication. A lengthy review that appeared under the initials C. M. L. mostly recounted the episodes in *Backfurrow* and noted the sympathetic characters are assailed by a "ruthless destiny" and that the novel "reminds one of a very honest woman, in black" (L, C.M. 4). Ruth Suckow, who had written an Iowa farm novel the year before, believed that *Backfurrow*, although convincing in general outline, lacked poignancy and truth in its details. She saved the devastating assessment of the protagonist for last, writing that "we have the uncomfortable suspicion that it was not circumstances, not his hard lot or even his poor beginning that defeated him" but Ralph's lack of intelligence (Suckow 4). The unsigned notice published in the *Times Literary Supplement* of the London printing of *Backfurrow* made the observation that the land has a vastly slower existence of its own than the farmers who labor in it, and concluded, "It is an able, though rather a depressing novel" (Review of *Backfurrow* 481). H. L. Mencken had high praise for *Backfurrow*, saying that it gave an "extraordinary vivid presentation of cruel, back-breaking toil" of running a farm and concluded, "Few first novels show so much seriousness or so much skill" (Mencken 125). Perhaps the most interesting and perceptive contemporary review of the novel was contributed by Donald Coney as part of a special issue on G. D. Eaton in the University of Michigan's student newspaper, the *Michigan Daily*. Coney, who seems to have known Eaton as an undergraduate, provided background and context that reveal that this was not the book expected from Eaton, a notorious campus provocateur and *bête noire*, and judged the mechanics, style, and literary quality to be disappointing. He pointed out that it is a first novel, and that although the observations are genuine, "he grows pedestrian and frequently awkward" (Coney 1). The *coup de grâce*, however, seems to have been delivered by Eaton's publisher, George Putnam himself. In an unattributed anecdote, David Anderson alleged that Putnam regretted issuing *Backfurrow* in the first place, even after some of the more objectionable sections had been deleted, and soon had it withdrawn from promotion and distribution (Anderson, "Michigan Proletarian" 85). If true, this explains why the book today is rather difficult to find in the antiquarian marketplace.

The same mixed reviews greeted Frederick's *Green Bush* when it appeared later in the fall. A surprisingly virulent notice by the Wisconsin writer Margery Latimer, whose mentor was Zona Gale, found little to praise and said that the author's prose was unexciting and apparently had no interest in achieving distinction in style; and that he "has said too much and implied too little, described too fully and evoked nothing at all" (Latimer 4). An anonymous reviewer for the *Saturday Review of Literature*, while acknowledging some weaknesses, found that the story did much to praise farm life instead of condemning it as full of "stupidity, barrenness and dullness" (Review of *Green Bush*, 26 Sept. 1925, 165). Another reviewer noted that it was an American story with American situations, and the author gradually described the attractiveness of rural Michigan, in spite of the drawbacks the protagonist experienced: "Mr. Frederick writes with feeling and he writes well" (Review of *Green Bush*, 14 Oct. 1925, 4).

With *Backfurrow* being suppressed by its publisher and *Green Bush* not seeing a second printing, both novels virtually disappeared from the literary scene for the next forty years. In 1965 Roy Meyer's important monograph *The Middle Western Farm Novel in the Twentieth Century* examined in detail 140 works of fiction published between 1891 and the early 1960s. He recognized the interesting comparisons and contrasts between the two 1925 farm novels set in Michigan and over the course of a few pages examined the implications of the use of the farm milieu that resulted in opposite outlooks. Looking at contemporary reviews and adding his own critical evaluations based on literary styles and biographical influences, Meyer concluded accurately, "If *Green Bush* qualifies as the strongest fictional defense of farm life, G.D. Eaton's *Backfurrow* ... must surely deserve to be called the bitterest attack on it" (Meyer 87). And lastly, "Ralph [Dutton]'s final position is far from the kind of optimistic acceptance that Frank Thompson achieves; it is a weary resignation to the inevitable, by a person too dulled and beaten by misfortune to struggle any longer" (Meyer 90).

As useful as Meyer's extended evaluation is, there are still some areas of comparison between *Backfurrow* and *Green Bush* that he has neglected or missed entirely that are worthy of mention. Both Ralph Dutton and Frank Thompson are only children. Illegitimate Ralph does not know his mother; she abandoned him to her parents as a baby. Frank's mother, a distinctly unsympathetic character, is "a most unusual vampire in gray silk" (Latimer 4). Both Ralph and Frank seek education: the former reads everything he can lay his hands on, but without context or understanding; Frank's education is from a university's formal sequence of courses and graduate work. Their respective wives are young women from farming families, have difficult pregnancies, and are silently reviled by their husbands when they prove to have hidden mental and physical strengths when called upon to run their farms. The seductive lure of the city is present in both novels, but much more so with Ralph's yearning for a better life in wealth, learning, and love; he fails to realize that the fleshpots, honky-tonks, and madding crowds of Detroit will never fulfill his wishes. Frank and Rose, however, recognize that city life is sterile and holds no future for them. Finally, the serious injuries that strike Ralph and Frank and their long recoveries set the courses for the novels' denouement: Ralph relies on his wife to make the farm viable, while Frank willingly gives up an academic career to remain with the land.

Roy Meyer characterizes *Backfurrow* and *Green Bush* as the nadir and zenith, respectively, of Michigan—and all of midwestern—farm fiction. Which is the truer picture of farming in the 1920s? If we remember that both Eaton and Frederick have themselves labored in the agricultural lands of Michigan at about the same time, their experiences are their own personal truths, with some literary embellishments. The answer to the question must be that both novels show accurately the different aspects of Michigan farm life of one hundred years ago as Eaton and Frederick individually experienced it.

Grand Valley State University, Emeritus

Note

1. Many online sources list G. D. Eaton's first name as "Geoffrey," but public and archival records indicate his name was actually "Godfrey." Biographical information about Godfrey Dell Eaton was compiled from US Census data and unpublished sources and ephemera from Eaton's student file among the alumni records held at the Bentley Historical Library, University of Michigan.

Works Cited and Consulted

Anderson, David D. "John T(owner) Frederick." *Dictionary of Midwestern Literature, Volume 1: The Authors*, edited by Philip A. Greasley, U Indiana P, 2001, pp. 203–04.

———. "Michigan Proletarian Writers and the Great Depression." *MidAmerica*, vol. 9, 1982, pp. 76–97.

Bush, Sargent, Jr. "The Achievement of John T. Frederick." *Books at Iowa*, vol. 14, no. 1, April 1971, pp. 8–30.

Coney, Donald. Review of *Backfurrow*. *The [University of] Michigan Daily*, 22 Feb. 1925, p. 1.

Eaton, G. D. *Backfurrow*. G. P. Putnam's Sons, 1925.

———. *John Drakin*. Gutenberg Publishing, 1937.

"Farm Literature." *Dictionary of Midwestern Literature, Volume 2: Dimensions of the Midwestern Literary Imagination*, edited by Philip A. Greasley, U Indiana P, 2016, pp. 237–43.

Frederick, John T. *Druida*. Alfred A. Knopf, 1923.

———. *Green Bush*. Alfred A. Knopf, 1925.

L., C. M. "*Backfurrow*: A Realistic Story of Life on a Michigan Farm." *Boston Evening Transcript*, 7 Mar. 1925, p. 4.

Latimer, Margery. "Man and the Soil." *New York Herald Tribune Books*, 27 Sept. 1925, p. 3.

Mencken, H. L. "Fiction." *American Mercury*, vol. 5, no. 17, May 1925, pp. 124–26.

Meyer, Roy W. *The Middle Western Farm Novel in the Twentieth Century*. U Nebraska P, 1965.

"The Midland." *Dictionary of Midwestern Literature, Volume 2: Dimensions of the Midwestern Literary Imagination*, edited by Philip A. Greasley, U Indiana P, 2016, pp. 494–96.

Reigelman, Milton M. "John T. Frederick." *The Palimpsest*, vol. 59, no. 2, Mar./Apr. 1978, pp. 58–65.

Review of *Backfurrow*. *Times Literary Supplement*, 16 July 1925, p. 481.

Review of *Green Bush*. *Boston Evening Transcript*, 14 Oct. 1925, p. 4.

Review of *Green Bush*. *Saturday Review of Literature*, vol. 2, no. 9, 26 Sept. 1925, pp. 164–65.

Suckow, Ruth. "Hostages to Fortune." *New York Tribune*, 8 Mar. 1925, p. 4.

FEATURED TO THE NATION
H. L. Mencken Promotes Midwestern Authors

Scott D. Emmert

For the number of notable books published that year, 1925 is widely recognized as a landmark in American literature. That authors from the Midwest are largely responsible for this standout year in American letters is less often acknowledged, however. The celebrated writers who published significant works one hundred years ago include F. Scott Fitzgerald, Ernest Hemingway, Willa Cather, Sinclair Lewis, Theodore Dreiser, Sherwood Anderson, John Dos Passos, Langston Hughes, and T. S. Eliot. That these writers were from the Midwest may not be known because their national reputations have eclipsed their regional origins. Of course, for these authors national distinction predates 1925, but in that year many of them had their status reinforced by arguably the nation's leading literary critic, H. L. Mencken. In reviews for *The American Mercury*, Mencken lauded novels by several midwestern authors to emphasize their national importance. His praise for these novels distinguished this extraordinary time in both American and midwestern literature as it was occurring. Today, Mencken's reviews suggest reasons for the continuing hold these works have on the national imagination, and they provide a benchmark against which changing critical views may be measured.

In 1923, near the start of the decade that would see his greatest celebrity and cultural influence and following a successful editorship of *The Smart Set*, Mencken—with George Jean Nathan and the backing of publisher Alfred A. Knopf—founded *The American Mercury*. Beginning publication in January 1924, with Mencken as editor for the next ten years, *The American Mercury* became "one of the leading intellectual journals in the nation" (Joshi 4). In his regular columns and book reviews for the magazine, Mencken extended his reach as the preeminent "literary and cultural arbiter of the twenties" (Gross 103). As one researcher puts it, "from his tower atop the *Mercury*, he was free to manipulate the gushing flow of literature in the United States" (Kloefkorn 11). By the end of 1925, circulation for *The American Mercury* stood at 75,000 (Mott 4). Moreover, its readers saw themselves as intellectually elite. Frank Luther Mott characterizes *The American Mercury* as "clearly planned for the more thoughtful reader of a free-thinking sort who had fifty cents to spend on a magazine in these inflationary years. For such a reader the contents of the new review were both intellectually exciting and to the last page entertaining" (4). Mencken could influence a significant portion of America's more serious readers, and his reviews placed books by midwestern writers at the forefront of the nation's literary consciousness.

Before 1925, Mencken had also expressed his appreciation for literature from the Midwest. In 1920, for example, in "The Literary Capital of the United States," a piece originally published in the British periodical *The Nation* and then reprinted in the United States,[1] Mencken called Chicago "at once the most hospitably cosmopolitan and the most thoroughly American of American cities" (92). Deriding New York City for its cultural pretensions and conformity, Mencken admired the unique "spirit" of Chicago for fostering almost every "serious" novelist "of the younger generation," naming Theodore Dreiser, Sherwood Anderson, Willa Cather, Booth Tarkington, and Henry B. Fuller (92). Three years later, in *The Smart Set*, Mencken again singled out the literary contributions of the Midwest when he commended *The Midland* as "probably the most influential literary periodical ever set up in America" ("Some New Books" 141).[2] John T. Frederick, founder and editor of *The Midland*, published primarily midwestern writers throughout the journal's run (1915–1933). In a letter to Frederick, Mencken enthused about the "excellent stuff" appearing in *The Midland*, and he allowed Frederick to use this praise to promote the magazine (Reigelman 20).

With writing by midwestern writers in his ken and with a national audience in mind, Mencken reviewed several of the most noteworthy novels published in 1925. These include *The Great Gatsby, The Professor's House, Arrowsmith,*

An American Tragedy, Dark Laughter, and *Manhattan Transfer.*[3] In addition, he reviewed books published that year by midwestern writers who today receive less attention, including Ruth Suckow, Walter J. Muilenberg, Carl Van Vechten, James Stevens, Geoffrey Dell Eaton, and Lee J. Smits. Although Mencken focused most often on fiction, he gave a passing glance to Langston Hughes and *The Weary Blues*[4] while spending more time discussing Alain Locke's edited collection *The New Negro.*

In 2025, no American novel was more celebrated in its centennial year than *The Great Gatsby.* In 1925, Mencken published two reviews of Fitzgerald's novel. A lengthy commentary appeared in the *Baltimore Evening Sun* on May 3rd, less than a month after *Gatsby* was published on April 10th. Subsequently reprinted in volumes of Fitzgerald criticism,[5] this review is likely well known. Two months later, in July, Mencken published a shorter take on Fitzgerald's latest novel in *The American Mercury.* In about three column inches, Mencken echoed ideas from his earlier piece, again insisting that Fitzgerald's improvement as a stylist rather than the book's characters or plot recommended *The Great Gatsby.* Whereas in previous works Fitzgerald displayed a mere "slipshod facility," Mencken found in *Gatsby's* style evidence of "a painstaking and conscientious artist" ("New Fiction" 382). Even though *The Great Gatsby* has been, and continues to be, the subject of deep scholarly inquiry into thematic and social aspects Mencken did not plumb, his recognition of the novel's stylistic beauty remains astute.

Likewise, Mencken admired the style of Cather's *The Professor's House* while questioning her "uncertain grasp of [novel] form" ("Fiction Good and Bad," 1925, 380). For him, the Tom Outland section "almost breaks the back of the story of Professor St. Peter." Nevertheless, Mencken praised highly Cather's style: "Her observation is sharp and exact; she is alert to the tragedy of every-day life; she sees her people, not in vacuums, but against a definite background; above all, she writes in clear, glowing and charming English. I know of no other American novelist, indeed, whose writing is so sure of its effects, and yet so free from artifice" (380). Mencken was so impressed by Cather's style that he employed rare exclamation points to conclude his review. Looking past the "[r]ather obvious" story, he positively enthused, "But how skillfully written! How excellent in its details! What an ingratiating piece of work!" (380). Today few readers, if any, would disagree with this final assessment.

In contrast to his views of *The Great Gatsby* and *The Professor's House*, Mencken celebrated Sinclair Lewis's *Arrowsmith* for both its form and substance. He began his long review of the novel by congratulating Lewis for his "technical skill." He elaborated: *Arrowsmith* "is not only an extremely engaging story, full of grotesque and devastating humors; it is also, in structure, the very model of a modern novel. It hangs together admirably. It moves, breathes, lives. From the first page to the last there is not the slightest faltering in direction or purpose" ("Arrowsmith" 507). Mencken also admired that clear purpose. He was fascinated by Lewis's dramatization of Martin Arrowsmith's "pursuit of truth" within "our highly materialistic society" that values science only for its commercial applications (507). Mencken welcomed Lewis's "preaching" against an educational and economic system that rewards "quacks" instead of scientists who work at "combating fraud and obscurantism" while "getting at and hymning the truth" (508). In our time when doubt is deliberately cast on the facts of history and science, Lewis's theme remains crucially relevant.

One of Mencken's most well-known reviews from this time is his essay on *An American Tragedy*. Long Dreiser's friend and supporter, Mencken has subsequently been charged with writing an unexpectedly malicious review,[6] as if he launched a torpedo at a looming hulk. *An American Tragedy* is perhaps the most tome-like novel in American letters, a book so long that it was first published in two volumes of about 200,000 words each. Mencken warned readers of the novel's great length in the very title of his review: "Dreiser in 840 Pages." The title suggests the tart tone in the assessment that followed. Although often seen as a hostile review, two qualifying points about it should be recognized. First, it barely dented its target as more than 50,000 copies of *An American Tragedy* were sold in the first year (Loving 318). Second, it is neither entirely negative nor stubbornly wrong-headed. Mencken, following his best critical practice, sought to sort out the novel's virtues from its transgressions. He began the review with surprise that Dreiser's latest novel was not better written. To Mencken, it appeared odd that despite its having been ten years since his last novel and with the reasonable expectation that "all his new customers" had a right to expect something different—"a book carefully designed and smoothly written, with no puerile cliches in it and no maudlin moralizing" ("Dreiser in 840 Pages" 379)— Dreiser persisted in his established ways. Moreover, the causes for the novel's length clearly annoyed Mencken. He called it a "shapeless and forbidding monster—a heaping cartload of raw materials for a novel, with rubbish of all sorts intermixed—a vast, sloppy, chaotic thing of 385,000 words—at least 250,000 of them unnecessary!" (379). He deplored Dreiser's often lifeless writing as "dreadful bilge" (380) and condemned his extended situations and scenes as full of "banal moralizing and trite, meaningless words" (380). Mencken found book one and the first parts of book two, which track protagonist Clyde Griffiths from St. Louis to Chicago to upstate New York as he rises in social class and materialistic ambition, to be especially tedious. So much so that in the end he quipped, "Hire your pastor to read the first volume for you" (381). Merciless? To be sure. But not personal. Dreiser's aesthetic had always relied on the weighty accretion of detail and not on light-footed prose, which more than one critic found vexing.

After excoriating Dreiser's prose style, however, Mencken then appreciated the overall effect of the novel. Noting a change in interest for readers beginning when Clyde murders Roberta Alden, Mencken thereafter saw "Dreiser at his plodding, booming best" (381). No longer "psychologizing" his characters' motivations, Dreiser sticks to describing their actions, "full of a sense of their helplessness." The result for Mencken was "superb" in that "[o]ne gets the same feeling of complete reality that came from 'Sister Carrie,' and especially from the last days of Hurstwood. The thing ceases to be a story, and becomes a harrowing reality" (381). In essence, Mencken praised the novel's ending for its powerful naturalism, for although the characters are "automata thrown hither and thither by fate" with "thoughts [that] are muddled and trivial," Dreiser "feels with them, and can make the reader feel with them." Mencken therefore admired Dreiser for a "skill … that is surely not common. Good writing is far easier" (381). Ultimately, Mencken urged the reading public not to "miss the second" volume of *An American Tragedy* for the grip of its "gradual, terrible, irresistible approach of doom" (381), for its stirring tragedy. In reviews of books published in 1925, Mencken often admired deft prose and truthful realism alike. His review of *An American Tragedy* should not be seen as singly vindictive because it was wholly consistent with his established judgment and recognizable taste.

Following this critical program, it is not surprising that Mencken admired several lesser-known novels by midwestern writers for their literary merit. Chief among these writers is Ruth Suckow, whom Mencken routinely celebrated. In Suckow's second novel,[7] *The Odyssey of a Nice Girl*, Mencken saw a thoroughly convincing portrait of "a typical girl in a small town of the Midlands—a girl almost mathematically normal" ("Fiction Good and Bad," 1926, 506). To Mencken, Suckow's style was "at once natural and highly artful. The tale does not boom along in scenes of high drama; it unfolds slowly, gradually" (506). Perceiving the novel's "fine feeling," Mencken nonetheless noted the "[i]rony [that] plays about it from first to last" though "always there is pity underneath" (507). This feeling and pity are central to Suckow's "delicate skill" as a writer—a skill with which she renders her protagonist, Marjorie Stoessel, with an understanding that Mencken found "genuinely moving" (507). For Mencken, the novel exemplified Suckow's ability to "discern and evoke the eternal tragedy in the life of man" (507). Mencken's preference for skillful writing and affective realism secured his praise for *The Odyssey of a Nice Girl*.

Mencken's admiration for writers who could render characters as emotionally credible also led him to recommend Sherwood Anderson's *Dark Laughter*, especially for its depiction of John Stockton, which Mencken thought was "brilliant and searching" ("Fiction Good and Bad," 1925, 380). Although he viewed Anderson's "manner" as possessing "defects, disadvantages, even absurdities," Mencken ultimately lauded Anderson's ability to "make his people breathe and move" (308). Similarly, Mencken appreciated two novels from 1925 set in Michigan. He found Geoffrey Dell Eaton's *Backfurrow* "moving" in its portrayal of "the life of a poor farmer in central Michigan" ("Fiction" 125), and he asserted that in *The Spring Flight* author Lee J. Smits presented "characters [who] are in the round and full of life" ("Fiction" 126). In contrast, yet with consistency, Mencken dismissed Carl Van Vechten's *Fire-Crackers* because the characters, or "marionettes" ("Fiction Good and Bad," 1925, 380) he saw as typical of Van Vechten's fiction were less amusing to him than before. More severely, he outright disliked Walter J. Muilenberg's *Prairie* for its "peasants … [that] never seem real to me for an instant" ("Fiction Good and Bad," 1925, 381). His sense of the authentic even informed his review of James Stevens's *Paul Bunyan*— which, although a fable, Mencken praised as "an American saga" and "epic" that "hymned as they deserved" the laborers who "cleared a continent" ("An American Saga" 254–55).

Mencken's ideas in these book reviews do not, of course, all bear up under examination. In fact, sometimes his views can be dismissed outright. For example, he scorned *Manhattan Transfer* as "incoherent and not infrequently dull" ("Fiction Good and Bad," 1926, 508) while offering no discussion of the novel whatsoever. Here he exhibited a bias against writers who enjoyed success with their first novels, as John Dos Passos did critically with *Three Soldiers* and Fitzgerald had commercially with *This Side of Paradise*. Egregiously, moreover, Mencken displayed a deplorable racism in his review of *The New Negro* edited by Alain Locke. In a piece titled "The Aframerican: New Style," he shamefully undercut his appreciation of "this dignified and impressive volume" and the contributors' "fierce sort of pride" (254) by trafficking in gross stereotypes. When writing of the "vast majority of the people of their race" whom he believed would not read Locke's collection, Mencken compared Blacks to "gorillas" who care only about "porkchops and bootleg gin" (255). Here Mencken made little effort to disguise his blatant prejudice. Indeed, he seemed to revel in it.

The frequent, scathing disapproval that Mencken unapologetically offered as legitimate, even seemingly as proof of his critical courage, colored his view of the actual Midwest. Although Mencken's reviews of books published in 1925 went a long way toward putting the Midwest on the literary map, his view of the region's small towns and rural expanses, and his sense of the people who lived in them, positioned the middle American states as a synecdoche for the nation's intellectual and cultural inferiority. Barry Gross writes that Mencken "saw the Midwest as America writ large, as the spiritual seat of everything that was most repressive and conventional, most drab and debilitating in American life" (103). To Mencken, the Midwest seemed deliberately dull and proudly provincial. In an essay on the poor steel towns outside Pittsburgh, a Midwest-adjacent city, he offhandedly scorned "the gloomy, God-forsaken villages of Iowa and Kansas" ("Libido" 190). Just as casually, he proffered a similar criticism in his review of *The Odyssey of a Nice Girl* when he commended Suckow for depicting "intimately" the "forlorn and soggy town" of Buena Vista, Iowa ("Fiction Good and Bad," 1926, 506). Even the region's urban centers could receive his back-handed condescension. By 1926, for example, Mencken's belief in the cultural superiority of Chicago had waned. Noting how writers such as Sherwood Anderson and Edgar Lee Masters had left the city, Mencken described them approvingly as "fugitive(s) from a Chicago in decay" ("Masters" 56). In the decade when airplanes were exotically familiar, Mencken presaged the later dismissal of the Midwest as mere "flyover country."

Nevertheless, it is not true, as Gross has asserted, that Mencken "greeted each new tome that came his way from [the Midwest] with a hoot of derision" (103). His expressed disdain for much of the Midwest did not bias him against writers from the region. In addition to positive reviews of midwestern novels, in *The American Mercury* he published short fiction by numerous writers from the Midwest, including not only Anderson, Dreiser, Fitzgerald, Hughes, Lewis, Suckow, and Stevens but also Thomas Boyd, James T. Farrell, Zona Gale, John Herrmann, Meridel LeSuer, Ferner Nuhn, and Jim Tully—as well as poetry by Vachel Lindsay, Edgar Lee Masters, and Carl Sandburg (Kloefkorn 13–23). Perhaps most surprising given his conservative political views, Mencken greatly assisted leftist proletarian writer Jack Conroy. As Jack Salzman notes, Mencken reviewed in mostly positive terms the 1930 issue of *Unrest*, an anthology Conroy co-edited, and he published in *The American Mercury* six sketches by Conroy, of which five were incorporated into his 1933 novel *The Disinherited* (525–26).

Mencken frequently promoted midwestern writers to a national readership. Of note is his celebration of authors from the Midwest whose books make 1925 a monument in American literature. The current critical esteem for the midwestern authors who published major works one hundred years ago may very well have an origin in H. L. Mencken's contemporaneous recognition of them.

University of Wisconsin—Oshkosh

Notes

1. In the *Chicago Daily News, Publishers' Weekly*, and in *On American Books*, a volume edited by Francis Hackett. See Joshi's bibliography, p. 78.

2. See also Reigelman, pp. 19–21.

3. Notably, he did not review *In Our Time*. Mencken's first review of a Hemingway book was of *Men without Women* in the May 1928 issue of *The American Mercury*.

4. In *The American Mercury*, Mencken devoted just two reviews to books of poetry, one appearing in October 1925 covering twenty-nine books and the other in June 1926 on sixty-one books ("Books of Verse"; Kloefkorn 24–25).

5. By Alfred Kazin in *F. Scott Fitzgerald: The Man and His Work* (1951); Matthew J. Bruccoli and Jackson R. Bryer in *F. Scott Fitzgerald in His Own Time: A Miscellany* (1971); and Jackson R. Bryer in *F. Scott Fitzgerald: The Critical Reception* (1978). See Joshi's bibliography, p. 246.

6. Jerome Loving notes that Mencken had promised to write a "polite" review of *An American Tragedy* before he took umbrage with Dreiser for his failure to ask about Mencken's sick mother (316–18).

7. Mencken called *The Odyssey of a Nice Girl* Suckow's "first full-length novel," finding her previous book, *Country People*, to be a "novelette, small in scale" (506).

Works Cited

Gross, Barry. "In Another Country: The Revolt from the Village." *MidAmerica*, vol. 4, 1977, pp. 101–11.

Joshi, S. T. Introduction. *H. L. Mencken: An Annotated Bibliography*. Scarecrow P, 2009, pp. 1–5.

Kloefkorn, Johnny L. "A Critical Study of the Work of H. L. Menchen [sic] as Literary Editor and Critic of *The American Mercury*." *The Emporia State Research Studies*, vol. 7, no. 4, June 1959, pp. 1–48.

Loving, Jerome. *The Last Titan: A Life of Theodore Dreiser*. U of California P, 2005.

Mencken, H. L. "The Aframerican: New Style." Review of *The New Negro: An Interpretation*. *The American Mercury*, vol. 7, no. 2, Feb. 1926, pp. 254–55.

———. "An American Saga." Review of *Paul Bunyan*. *The American Mercury*, vol. 5, no. 2, June 1925, pp. 254–55.

———. "Arrowsmith." Review of *Arrowsmith*. *The American Mercury*, vol. 4, no. 4, Apr. 1925, pp. 507–09.

———. "Books of Verse." Review of *The Weary Blues*. *The American Mercury*, vol. 8, no. 2, June 1926, pp. 251–54.

———. "Dreiser in 840 Pages." Review of *An American Tragedy*. *The American Mercury*, vol. 7, no. 3, Mar. 1926, pp. 379–81.

———. "Fiction." Review of *Backfurrow* and *The Spring Flight*. *The American Mercury*, vol. 5, no. 1, May 1925, pp. 124–26.

———. "Fiction Good and Bad." Review of *Dark Laughter, The Professor's House, Fire-Crackers*, and *Prairie*. *The American Mercury*, vol. 6, no. 3, Nov. 1925, pp. 379–83.

———. "Fiction Good and Bad." Review of *The Odyssey of a Nice Girl* and *Manhattan Transfer*. *The American Mercury*, vol. 7, no. 4, Apr. 1926, pp. 506–09.

———. "The Libido for the Ugly." *Prejudices: Sixth Series*, Knopf, 1927, pp. 187–93.

———. "The Literary Capital of the United States." *The Nation*, vol. 27, no. 3, 17 Apr. 1920, pp. 90, 92.

———. "Masters." *Prejudices: Fifth Series*, Knopf, 1926, pp. 56–63.

———. "New Fiction." Review of *The Great Gatsby. The American Mercury*, vol. 5, no. 3, July 1925, pp. 382–83.

———. "Some New Books." *The Smart Set,* vol. 71, no. 3, July 1923, pp. 138–44.

Mott, Frank Luther. *A History of American Magazines: Sketches of 21 Magazines, 1905–1930*, vol. 5. Harvard UP, 1968.

Reigelman, Milton M. *The Midland: A Venture in Literary Regionalism.* U of Iowa P, 1975.

Salzman, Jack. "Conroy, Mencken, and *The American Mercury.*" *Journal of Popular Culture*, vol. 7, no. 3, winter 1973, pp. 524–28.

Society for the Study of **MIDWESTERN LITERATURE**

2026 Symposium of Scholars and Creative Writers

CALL FOR PROPOSALS
• papers/posters • panels • round tables

LITERARY CRITICISM or CREATIVE WRITING or PEDAGOGY

See ssml.org for submission instructions.

DEADLINE February 15, 2026

QUESTIONS Jeff Hotz (jhotz@esu.edu)

MAY 28–29 2026

WRITING THE MIDWEST
Kellogg Hotel and Convention Center • East Lansing, MI

CFP: Reading and Writing the Midwest

Recent essays in popular publications such as *The Atlantic*, *The New York Times*, and *Psychology Today* have sounded the alarm that college students today cannot read. Is this true? The Society for the Study of Midwestern Literature calls for proposals for an upcoming issue of its peer-reviewed journal *Midwestern Miscellany* devoted to the topic of Reading and Writing the Midwest, to be guest-edited by Rachael Price (Abraham Baldwin Agricultural College) and Catherine Clifford (Hastings College).

Successful essays will describe a specific challenge in the classroom and/or a successful classroom activity or assignment; evaluate a theory of reading, writing, literacy, or pedagogy; or examine a text or historical moment related to literacy in the Midwest. Please send proposals (max. 300 words) and short CV to Catherine Clifford (cat.clifford@hastings.edu) and Rachael Price (rprice @abac.edu) by March 1, 2026. Finished essays should be 3,000-6,000 words.

Topics may include, but are not limited to, the following:

- Classroom exercises or lesson plans that engage Midwestern students in reading and/or writing
- Midwestern texts that engage students or promote specific reading skills
- Writing about the Midwest or place
- Responses to think pieces about university students and reading and/or writing
- Debates about early reading instruction (such as the Science of Reading and/or Whole Language reading)
- Theories of literacy, as they apply to midwestern classrooms and/or texts
- Theories of composition, including multimodal composition and accessibility, as they apply to midwestern classrooms and/or texts
- Use of generative AI in higher ed classrooms
- Theories of evaluation, such as anti-racist or equity-minded grading, in higher ed
- Debates about school choice, charter schools, or parents' rights bills in the Midwest

*AI-generated image of Midwestern higher ed classroom with laptops.

New Perspectives on Midwestern Working-Class Literature

The Society for the Study of Midwestern Literature invites essay proposals for an upcoming issue of its peer-reviewed journal *Midwestern Miscellany* on the topic of Midwestern Working-Class Literature, to be guest edited by Marilyn Atlas (atlas@ohio.edu). *Midwestern working-class literature* is a genre of writing that focuses on the lives and experiences of working-class people living in the American Midwest, exploring themes of industrial and farm labor, economic hardship, community struggle, and social issues prevalent in the region.

Douglas Wixson, in *Worker-Writer in America* (1994), demonstrates a tradition of twentieth-century Midwestern literary radicalism. Writers in this tradition include notable authors such as Hamlin Garland (*Main-Travelled Roads*), Upton Sinclair (*The Jungle*), Richard Wright (*Native Son*), Theodore Dreiser (*Sister Carrie*), Tillie Olsen (*Tell Me a Riddle*), Toni Morrison (*The Bluest Eye*), and Sanora Babb (*whose names are unknown*). But the field has expanded to include previously ignored communities and print forms, such as hobo newspapers and Heartland Marxist magazines, as well.

For this issue, SSML seeks new and diverse approaches to the study of Midwestern working-class literature. Potential contributors are invited to propose creative topics on well-known writers/texts or to expand or challenge the established history or conventions of working-class literature in the Midwest. Questions might include, but are not limited to, the following: What is the role of the working-class writer in working-class literature? Is this literature diverse, hybrid, or experimental? How has the literary representation of labor changed over time?

Please send queries and/or proposals to Marilyn Atlas (atlas@ohio.edu) by March 1, 2026. Proposals should be no more than 700 words and should be accompanied by a recent CV. (Finished essays should be 3,000-6,000 words.)

Call for Proposals

The Society for the Study of Midwestern Literature invites essay proposals for a forthcoming issue of the peer-reviewed journal Midwestern Miscellany on the topic of Midwestern Drama, to be guest-edited by Marilyn Atlas (atlas@ohio.edu).

Recent years have seen a resurgence of interest in Midwestern drama. In 2022, for example, Marcia Noe published *Three Midwestern Playwrights: How Floyd Dell, George Cram Cook, and Susan Glaspell Transformed American Theatre*, a critical work highlighting the importance of the Midwest in forging Modernist American theater. Several classic Midwestern plays have recently been revived or reevaluated, such as Lorraine Hansberry's *The Sign in Sidney Brustein's Window* (New York) and Arthur Miller's *All My Sons* (London), with its radical color-blind casting and earthy toned, "Midwest" staging. And Noah Diaz's *You Will Get Sick* (performed at the Steppenwolf in Chicago 2025) shows us something hilarious and brilliant about Midwesterners and the contemporary Midwest economic scene. It is time for scholars to weigh in again and reinterpret Midwest drama from a fresh perspective.

Contributors may address any aspect of Midwestern drama (i.e., drama set or performed in the Midwest), but topics might include the following:

- Still little-known Midwest dramatists that ought to be getting attention
- Important Midwestern plays that have been ignored or forgotten
- Verse dramas (such as Harriet Monroe's) that deserve a second look
- Contemporary Midwestern drama, troupes, or theatre spaces
- Dramatists or plays that challenge traditional conceptions or narratives of the Midwest
- New theoretical or critical approaches to well-known Midwestern plays or dramatists
- Revivals of Midwestern plays

Please send queries and/or proposals to Marilyn Atlas (atlas@ohio.edu) by March 1, 2026. Proposals should be no more than 700 words and should be accompanied by a recent CV. (Finished essays should be 3,000-6,000 words.)

Image: Screenshot of trailer for Noah Diaz's *You Will Get Sick*, Steppenwolf Theatre (Chicago, IL), June 5 to July 20, 2025 (Andrew Boyce, scenic design).